OPPOSING
VIEWPOINTS®
SERIES

RA643 .F

Resurgent diseases

Resurgent Diseases

Other Books of Related Interest:

Opposing Viewpoints Series

Bioterrorism

Current Controversies Series

Vaccines

At Issue Series

Pandemics

"Congress shall make no law. . .abridging the freedom of speech, or of the press."

First Amendment to the U.S. Constitution

The basic foundation of our democracy is the First Amendment guarantee of freedom of expression. The *Opposing Viewpoints* Series is dedicated to the concept of this basic freedom and the idea that it is more important to practice it than to enshrine it.

OPPOSING
VIEWPOINTS®
SERIES

Resurgent Diseases

Karen Miller, Book Editor

GREENHAVEN PRESS
A part of Gale, Cengage Learning

GALE
CENGAGE Learning™

Detroit • New York • San Francisco • New Haven, Conn • Waterville, Maine • London

Christine Nasso, *Publisher*
Elizabeth Des Chenes, *Managing Editor*

© 2009 Greenhaven Press, a part of Gale, Cengage Learning

Gale and Greenhaven Press are registered trademarks used herein under license.

For more information, contact:
Greenhaven Press
27500 Drake Rd.
Farmington Hills, MI 48331-3535
Or you can visit our Internet site at gale.cengage.com

For product information and technology assistance, contact us at

Gale Customer Support, 1-800-877-4253
For permission to use material from this text or product, submit all requests online at
www.cengage.com/permissions

Further permissions questions can be emailed to permissionrequest@cengage.com

Articles in Greenhaven Press anthologies are often edited for length to meet page requirements. In addition, original titles of these works are changed to clearly present the main thesis and to explicitly indicate the author's opinion. Every effort is made to ensure that Greenhaven Press accurately reflects the original intent of the authors. Every effort has been made to trace the owners of copyrighted material.

Cover image © George Doyle/Stockbyte/Getty Images.

LIBRARY OF CONGRESS CATALOGING-IN-PUBLICATION DATA

Resurgent diseases / Karen Miller, book editor.
   p. cm. -- (Opposing viewpoints)
  Includes bibliographical references and index.
  ISBN 978-0-7377-4228-2 (hardcover)
  ISBN 978-0-7377-4229-9 (pbk.)
  1. Emerging infectious diseases. I. Miller, Karen, 1973-
  RA643.R42 2009
  362.196'9--dc22

                       2008033989

Printed in the United States of America
1 2 3 4 5 6 7 12 11 10 09 08

Contents

Chapter 3: How Can Resurgent Diseases Be Controlled?

Chapter 4: How Can Disease Resurgence Be Reduced?

Why Consider
Opposing Viewpoints?

> *"The only way in which a human being can make some approach to knowing the whole of a subject is by hearing what can be said about it by persons of every variety of opinion and studying all modes in which it can be looked at by every character of mind. No wise man ever acquired his wisdom in any mode but this."*
>
> John Stuart Mill

In our media-intensive culture it is not difficult to find differing opinions. Thousands of newspapers and magazines and dozens of radio and television talk shows resound with differing points of view. The difficulty lies in deciding which opinion to agree with and which "experts" seem the most credible. The more inundated we become with differing opinions and claims, the more essential it is to hone critical reading and thinking skills to evaluate these ideas. *Opposing Viewpoints* books address this problem directly by presenting stimulating debates that can be used to enhance and teach these skills. The varied opinions contained in each book examine many different aspects of a single issue. While examining these conveniently edited opposing views, readers can develop critical thinking skills such as the ability to compare and contrast authors' credibility, facts, argumentation styles, use of persuasive techniques, and other stylistic tools. In short, the *Opposing Viewpoints* series is an ideal way to attain the higher-level thinking and reading skills so essential in a culture of diverse and contradictory opinions.

In addition to providing a tool for critical thinking, *Opposing Viewpoints* books challenge readers to question their own strongly held opinions and assumptions. Most people form their opinions on the basis of upbringing, peer pressure, and personal, cultural, or professional bias. By reading carefully balanced opposing views, readers must directly confront new ideas as well as the opinions of those with whom they disagree. This is not to simplistically argue that everyone who reads opposing views will—or should—change his or her opinion. Instead, the series enhances readers' understanding of their own views by encouraging confrontation with opposing ideas. Careful examination of others' views can lead to the readers' understanding of the logical inconsistencies in their own opinions, perspective on why they hold an opinion, and the consideration of the possibility that their opinion requires further evaluation.

Evaluating Other Opinions

To ensure that this type of examination occurs, *Opposing Viewpoints* books present all types of opinions. Prominent spokespeople on different sides of each issue as well as well-known professionals from many disciplines challenge the reader. An additional goal of the series is to provide a forum for other, less known, or even unpopular viewpoints. The opinion of an ordinary person who has had to make the decision to cut off life support from a terminally ill relative, for example, may be just as valuable and provide just as much insight as a medical ethicist's professional opinion. The editors have two additional purposes in including these less known views. One, the editors encourage readers to respect others' opinions—even when not enhanced by professional credibility. It is only by reading or listening to and objectively evaluating others' ideas that one can determine whether they are worthy of consideration. Two, the inclusion of such viewpoints encourages the important critical thinking skill of objectively evaluating an author's credentials and bias. This evaluation will illuminate an author's reasons for taking a particular stance on an issue and will aid in readers' evaluation of the author's ideas.

It is our hope that these books will give readers a deeper understanding of the issues debated and an appreciation of the complexity of even seemingly simple issues when good and honest people disagree. This awareness is particularly important in a democratic society such as ours in which people enter into public debate to determine the common good. Those with whom one disagrees should not be regarded as enemies but rather as people whose views deserve careful examination and may shed light on one's own.

Thomas Jefferson once said that "difference of opinion leads to inquiry, and inquiry to truth." Jefferson, a broadly educated man, argued that "if a nation expects to be ignorant and free. . .it expects what never was and never will be." As individuals and as a nation, it is imperative that we consider the opinions of others and examine them with skill and discernment. The *Opposing Viewpoints* series is intended to help readers achieve this goal.

David L. Bender and Bruno Leone,
Founders

Introduction

"Most people believe that victory over the major infectious diseases of the last century came with the invention of immunizations. In fact, cholera, typhoid fever, tetanus, diphtheria, whooping cough, and others were in decline before vaccines for them became available—the result of better methods of sanitation, sewage disposal, and distribution of food and water." —Andrew Weil

For most people in the United States, measles is an annoying disease that causes an itchy rash and runny eyes, sometimes accompanied by a fever for a couple of days. Of course, there are exceptions. Adults who catch the disease suffer more often from serious complications, such as diarrhea or pneumonia. In the worst cases, victims of measles can lose their eyesight, although such extreme reactions are very rare. The fatality rate from measles in developed nations is 0.1 percent. Worldwide, however, measles is much more serious. Fatality rates in the general population of underdeveloped nations average about 10 percent; among people who are already sick or immunocompromised in some way, the rate is as high as 30 percent.

Fortunately for Americans today, the nation's economic prosperity allows for a population in generally good health. According to Denise Grady, the author of the *New York Times* story, "Measles in U.S. at Highest Level Since 2001" (May 2, 2008), annually measles killed more than four hundred children and hospitalized forty-eight thousand before 1963, the year the measles vaccine became available in the United States. After almost forty years of medical efforts and easy access to the vaccine, the transmission of measles within the United States ended in 2000, Grady reports. Since then, nonetheless, several outbreaks have occurred across the country, usually triggered by the return of a visitor abroad who lacked immunity to the disease and brought it home, infecting other people who lacked immunity. The disease can spread to others for almost two weeks before the carrier becomes sick. Americans have been lucky that it has only been measles outbreaks so far, instead of something deadlier.

What has changed since 2000? People have been traveling between continents since long before that. Because measles treatment usually involves managing symptoms rather than attacking the virus directly, measles has not developed significant resistance to medications. One possible explanation points to declining immunity rates. Measles has been nearly eradicated, so it does not seem like a pressing threat. Current parents of young children are too young themselves to remember how widespread measles used to be and have few personal reasons to fear it. Even with the latest resurgence, an individual's chances of catching the disease are low, and the chances of suffering dangerous complications even lower. From that perspective, skipping a vaccine or a booster appointment is just not that big of a deal. Although the measles vaccine is officially required to enroll children in public school, forty-eight of fifty states allow exemptions for a variety of reasons, often religious ones.

Also consider the current controversy surrounding the measles vaccine: Some years ago, the vaccine was delivered in a solution that contained the preservative thimerosal, which contains a form of mercury and has lately been blamed for a purported rise in autism rates. In autism support groups and online vaccination message boards, parents share stories of bright babies and toddlers who reacted to routine vaccinations by developing neurological problems. The actress Jenny McCarthy is probably the most famous of such parents; she has popularized the issue and spoken out against vaccines in very public forums, with a published book and an appearance on Oprah Winfrey's talk show.

Scientific studies repeatedly fail to find any link between autism and thimerosal, but parents are still suspicious. Perhaps thimerosal is serving as a scapegoat for a collection of fears about vaccines and the harm they have been shown to cause. Sometimes a vaccine causes the disease it is intended to prevent. Sometimes a person has an adverse reaction to a vaccine and suffers lasting injury; the United States government has established the Vaccine Adverse Event Reporting System and even founded the National Vaccine Injury Compensation Program to manage this real, albeit rare, problem. Vaccine developers and manufacturers—frequently large international companies worth billions of dollars—are not always considered trustworthy, either. According to Ayodele Samuel Jegede in the March 2007 issue of *PLoS Medicine*, behind the mass rejection of the polio vaccine in Nigeria was the belief that the Pfizer corporation had conducted unethical experiments on African children in the 1990s (cited in a 2001 lawsuit filed in New York City). In addition, concerned individuals wonder if vaccines are really safe. In the United States, the chances of catching a particular disease are in most cases much greater than the chances of suffering an adverse effect to its vaccine.

When vaccination programs break down, vanishing diseases find new footholds in populations. Still, even successful vaccine programs are not impenetrable barriers to infection— any societal or environmental change can present new opportunities for a disease to reestablish itself. *Opposing Viewpoints: Resurgent Diseases* presents the debate in the following chapters: What Causes Disease Resurgence? How Should Society Respond to Resurgent Diseases? How Can Resurgent Diseases Be Controlled? and How Can Disease Resurgence Be Reduced? The authors of the collected viewpoints address and debate the factors contributing to disease resurgence and examine the social, ethical, medical, and technological aspects of this multifaceted problem.

OPPOSING
VIEWPOINTS®
SERIES

CHAPTER 1

What Causes Disease Resurgence?

Chapter Preface

From 1999 to 2006, a community in the African nation of Ivory Coast suffered from repeated outbreaks of a disease that manifested as symptoms in 92 percent of inhabitants and had a fatality rate of 20 percent. The community? A group of chimpanzees. The disease? A *human* respiratory virus.

Zoonoses are diseases that transmit from animals to humans, or vice versa. That a disease could infect both chimpanzees and humans is hardly surprising considering the two species' genetic similarity, but many diseases make the jump between more distantly related species all the time: rabies, toxoplasmosis, bird flu, anthrax, and plague are transmitted to humans by common animals such as bats, cats, chickens, cows, and rodents respectively.

One reason that zoonotic diseases resurge is that the pathogens can "hide" inside animal populations even as humans are eradicating it from their own communities. Another reason is that, as human populations increase in size, they expand into animals' territories, forcing more human-animal interactions and providing new opportunities for these diseases to infect people. Disease resurgence, however, is not unique to zoonoses. Diseases mutate so that medicines are no longer effective against them; vaccination campaigns fail and diseases creep back into populations; social institutions collapse and destroy technologies and infrastructure that held diseases at bay; social habits and beliefs change, leaving people vulnerable to new infections.

Occasionally, infection is not even required to trigger new outbreaks of old diseases. Rickets, for example, is seen in children who have a deficiency of vitamin D. A 2006 outbreak of fifty-nine cases in Oakland, California, was attributed to a set of factors: the babies had been breastfed (breast milk does not contain vitamin D) and the babies had darker skin that absorbed less sunlight (sun exposure is a source of vitamin D). Because of the benefits of breastfeeding, rates of formula feeding (formula has vitamin D) are dropping, and American life is happening indoors more often than out—these two factors both contribute to the rise of a disease the health care industry had nearly eradicated in the 1930s. When rickets was prevalent, parents knew how to ward it off (oftentimes by administering daily spoonfuls of cod liver oil). After rickets vanished from popular awareness, ordinary people forgot how to protect themselves.

Microscopic though they may be, bacteria, fungi, and—to a significant extent—viruses are living things with the same biological impetus to survive that compels all species to endure and reproduce. Life adapts to hostile environments and develops innate protection against infectious agents. Somewhere along the way, for example, humans' ancestors with sickle-cell anemia became less susceptible to malaria. But as a species evolves to resist disease, pathogenic species evolve to bypass protective adaptations. The bacteria *staphylococcus aureus*, for example, became resistant to penicillin, then to tetracycline, and then to erythromycin. Humans will develop new medicines and fight the diseases; future generations of bacteria will become immune to their effects and reappear in great numbers. The cycle of disease suppression and resurgence is a fact of life.

The following chapter explores the mechanisms and environments that promote the resurgence of diseases and the strategies people have developed to prevent and control them.

> *"The ultimate determinant of dengue prevalence in this setting is socioeconomic rather than environmental."*

Socioeconomic Factors Cause Disease Resurgence

Paul Reiter et al.

Paul Reiter is a professor of medical entomology at the Pasteur Institute in Paris, France, before which he worked at the United States Centers for Disease Control and Prevention for more than twenty years. He specializes in the study of mosquito-borne diseases, such as malaria and dengue fever. In the following viewpoint, Reiter and his colleagues describe the prevalence of dengue fever in two cities—one American, one Mexican—separated only by a river, the Rio Grande. Because their geography and climate are identical, Reiter credits socioeconomic differences for the rarity of the disease in Texas when it is common in Mexico.

As you read, consider the following questions:

1. What characteristics do the cities of Laredo, Texas, and Nuevo Laredo in Mexico have in common, according to Reiter and his colleagues?

Paul Reiter et al., "Texas Lifestyle Limits Transmission of Dengue Virus," *Emerging Infectious Diseases*, vol. 9, no. 1, January 2003, pp. 86–89. www.cdc.gov.

2. What building feature greatly reduces the transmission of the dengue virus by mosquitoes, in the authors' opinion?

3. Reiter and his colleagues speculate that global warming will affect the transmission of the dengue virus in the United States in what way?

Outbreaks of mosquito-borne infection are commonly assumed to occur wherever competent vectors [carriers] and a suitable climate exist, and that "global warming"— climate change caused by human activities—will cause these diseases to move to higher altitudes and latitudes. In many parts of the world, however, such diseases have become uncommon, despite an abundance of vectors and an ideal climate.

Denguelike illness was first noted in the New World as a major outbreak in Philadelphia in 1780, and similar episodes occurred in the United States for more than 150 years. In 1922, the disease struck many major cities in the southern states, including an estimated 500,000 cases in Texas. Another widespread outbreak occurred in 1947–48. In the past 50 years, however, autochthonous [indigenous] cases have been rare, despite an abundance of *Aedes aegypti* [mosquitoes] in the southeastern United States, and the arrival of millions of travelers from neighboring countries where the disease is endemic. From 1980 to 1999, only 64 locally acquired cases were confirmed in Texas, whereas 62,514 suspected cases were recorded in three adjoining Mexican states—Coahuila, Nuevo León, and Tamaulipas. In the same period, immigration authorities reported [less than or equal to] 70 million personal crossings from these states into Texas in a single year. Thus, the international border separates a dengue-endemic region from one in which the disease is rare.

Laredo, Texas, United States (population 200,000), and Nuevo Laredo, Taumalipas, Mexico (population 289,000), are essentially a single city (locally known as "los dos Laredos") divided by a small river, the Rio Grande. The rapid growth of this metropolitan area—70% in the past decade—is mainly due to massive cross-border traffic across three multi-lane bridges. In the summer of 1999, toward the end of a local dengue outbreak, we conducted a seroepidemiologic survey [a test for antibodies in the blood] to examine factors affecting dengue transmission on both sides of the border.

Collecting Data

Households were selected by a modified version of the cluster survey of the World Health Organization Expanded Program on Immunization. First, we mapped the population of each census block in Laredo and in a major portion of Nuevo Laredo (Sector 1). In each city, 30 clusters were chosen from these census blocks by using a selection probability proportional to population. Four city blocks were randomly chosen from each of these clusters, and individual houses in one or more of those blocks were selected at random (where block maps were available) or systematically from a randomly chosen starting point. Blocks were sampled until 7–12 households had been enrolled from each cluster.

Binational teams, each composed of an epidemiologist, a nurse, and an entomologist, conducted the surveys. A blood sample was obtained by fingerstick from a randomly selected resident (ages 18–65). A short questionnaire solicited general household information (number of inhabitants, type of construction, proximity to neighboring houses, number of bedrooms, presence and type of air-cooling system, and the presence and quality of window screens). Demographic data and travel histories of the blood donors were also recorded. Yards and patios were searched for *Ae. aegypti* breeding sites. . . .

Comparing Two Cities

Surveys were completed in 622 households (309 in Laredo, 313 in Nuevo Laredo), and 516 persons (228 in Laredo, 288 in

High Standard of Living Prevents Epidemics

Essentially, the [Laredo] study illustrates the importance of a vigorous economy and high standards of living to prevent dengue and other important insect-borne diseases. The same is true of our protections against malaria. Many malaria-infected people are reported in the United States each year. For example, over 1,300 imported cases were documented in 2002 and this does not accurately account for many unreported cases that occur in illegal workers. In spite of a continuous flow of malaria infections into the U.S., our country does not have endemic malaria. We have sustained this relative freedom from malaria for almost 60 years. Yet, we maintain almost no response capability to an imported case or exercise any specific preventive measures. Our freedom of malaria is not because of cold U.S. temperatures, use of insecticides or anti-malaria drugs, or any other specific malaria preventive measure. No, our freedom from malaria is a direct result of wealth and high standards of living. Indeed, a high standard of living is far and away the best malaria preventive measure yet discovered.

Don Roberts,
U.S. Senate Committee on Environment and Public Works,
October 23, 2007.

Nuevo Laredo) provided blood samples. IgM seropositivity [presence of anti-dengue antibody IgM] was lower in Laredo than in Nuevo Laredo. IgG seropositivity [presence of anti-dengue antibody IgG] was also lower in Laredo. Conversely, mosquito-infested containers were more abundant on the Texas side of the border: the Breteau Index (the number of infested containers per 100 houses) was 91 in Laredo versus

37 in Nuevo Laredo. Eighty-two percent of homes in Laredo had central or room air-conditioning versus 24% in Nuevo Laredo. In Laredo, evaporative coolers (a low-technology air-conditioning device that cools and humidifies air by drawing it from outdoors through a continually wetted screen) were less prevalent, a greater proportion of houses had intact screens, the average distance between houses was greater, and fewer persons lived in each house.

Analysis indicated a significant association between IgM seropositivity and five variables: absence of air-conditioning, fewer room air-conditioning units, the presence of an evaporative cooler, no travel outside the Laredo/Nuevo Laredo area, and shorter distances to neighboring houses. IgG seropositivity was significantly associated with absence of central air-conditioning, fewer room air-conditioning units, smaller plot size, and a shorter distance to neighboring houses.

Backward selection of variables yielded two that remained significantly associated with IgM seropositivity: absence of air-conditioning and no history of travel beyond Laredo/Nuevo Laredo in the previous 3 months. IgG seropositivity was associated with absence of air-conditioning, a history of crossing the border during the previous 3 months, and a greater number of occupants per household. . . . The proportion of dengue infections attributable to lack of air-conditioning in Nuevo Laredo was 55%, i.e., 55% of cases of dengue in Nuevo Laredo would not have occurred if all households in Nuevo Laredo had air-conditioning.

Similar Climate, Dissimilar Lifestyles

Given the proximity of the two cities, the difference in transmission rates cannot be attributed to climate. Moreover, the mean daily temperature for August, the peak month of transmission, was 32.2°C, several degrees higher than the mean for the hottest months on Caribbean islands where dengue is common. Indeed, summer temperatures throughout the range of *Ae. aegypti* in the southern United States are hotter than in many tropical regions where the disease is endemic.

Despite mosquito control campaigns on both sides of the border, *Ae. aegypti* infestation rates in Laredo were remarkably high. The Breteau Index was on a par with that observed during major dengue epidemics in Puerto Rico. The House Index (the percentage of houses with at least one infested container) was 37%, seven times higher than the level (5%) equated with a "high risk" of dengue transmission by the World Health Organization. Thus, vector [mosquito] populations cannot account for the low rate of transmission on the Texas side of the border.

Ae. aegypti is closely associated with human habitation and readily enters buildings to feed and to rest during periods of inactivity. In this context, casual observation supported the association of lack of air-conditioning with dengue transmission. In Laredo, most shops, restaurants and other public places are air conditioned and have closed windows and self-closing doors, as do houses in residential areas, even in low income neighborhoods. By contrast, in Nuevo Laredo, many shops, bars, and restaurants are open to the street, and the windows and doors of houses are left open, particularly in the daytime. Thus, there is less opportunity for mosquito/human contact in Laredo than in the Mexican city.

More than 85% of all buildings in Texas are fully air conditioned. Indeed, air-conditioning is ubiquitous in many parts of the United States. To maximize heating/cooling efficiency, windows are usually fully glazed and are often kept permanently closed. Thus, most people spend much of their daily life sequestered in sealed buildings. Even if infected mosquitoes gain entry to such buildings, the artificially dry atmosphere lowers their survival rate, and the cool temperature extends the extrinsic incubation period, reducing the likelihood of transmission. Presumably, when denied access to humans, mosquitoes must seek other hosts. In Puerto Rico and Thailand, some *Ae. aegypti* feed on dogs, even when humans are readily accessible. In Laredo, we observed that large dogs were housed in outdoor kennels at many homes. Whether these animals are an important blood source for the species would be an interesting topic for future research.

The dollar cost of electricity is similar in Laredo and Nuevo Laredo, but income, as indicated by per capita gross domestic product, is much higher in Texas than in Taumalipas. The proportional cost of maintaining air-conditioning for an entire dengue season is therefore much higher for the average family in Mexico and is unaffordable for the majority. Thus, the ultimate determinant of dengue prevalence in this setting is socioeconomic rather than environmental.

Humans Can Adapt

It has frequently been stated that dengue, malaria, and other mosquito-borne diseases will become common in the United States as a result of global warming. Such predictions often refer to vectorial capacity, a simple model that incorporates the population density, biting frequency, and daily survival probability of the vector, and the extrinsic incubation period of the pathogen. Although the vectorial capacity model has proved useful for interpreting entomo[insect]-epidemiologic data, particularly for transmission of malaria, it does not incorporate factors like air-conditioning, use of evaporative coolers, and the behavior of mosquitoes and humans. If the current warming trend in world climates continues, air-conditioning may become even more prevalent in the United States, in which case, the probability of dengue transmission is likely to decrease. If the economy of Mexico continues to grow, the use of air-conditioners may gain momentum south of the border.

| "The reason polio has endured is not because of the tenacity of the virus. It's politics."

Politics Cause Disease Resurgence

Chris Hondros

Chris Hondros is a Pulitzer Prize–nominated photojournalist. He has photographed people and scenes in most of the world's major conflict zones since the late 1990s, from eastern Europe, Africa, and the Middle East to Asia. His work has appeared on the covers of major news magazines and the front pages of major newspapers. The following viewpoint is his account of a visit to the Nigerian city of Kano. He details the political and social environment that disrupted the distribution of polio vaccine in the northern part of the country and the effects of the disease upon individuals who contract it.

As you read, consider the following questions:

1. What goal was set by the World Health Organization in 1988, as reported by Hondros?

2. What rumors about the polio vaccine were spread in the northern parts of Nigeria, according to the author?

Chris Hondros, "Polio Rebounds in Nigeria," *Digital Journalist*, vol. 91, May 2005. http://digitaljournalist.org. Reproduced by permission.

3. As described by Hondros, in what way is a child vaccinated against polio?

It all seemed so possible in 1988.

That was when the World Health Organization [WHO] and other international health groups set the year 2000 as its target to totally eliminate polio from the face of the Earth, later amending the date to 2005. Polio eradication back then seemed ambitious but doable. Health groups were still awash in the glow of eradicating smallpox a decade earlier, and a new, cheap polio vaccine that could be widely distributed over rural areas enabled easier-than-ever mass inoculations. Hope was in the air.

But 2005—the 50th anniversary of the approval of Jonas Salk's famous vaccine—has arrived with polio far from eradicated. In fact it's on the march again, with hundreds of new cases in northern Nigeria alone [in 2004]; infections from Nigeria have spread, reaching as far as Indonesia. But the reason polio has endured is not because of the tenacity of the virus. It's politics—post 9/11 politics.

I saw this for myself during a visit to Nigeria's regional capital of Kano [in April 2005]. Kano is a dusty and historic crossroads that once marked the beginning of trade and civilization for trans-Saharan travelers. During the harmattan season [characterized by hot, dry winds], the brown earthen buildings are sandblasted with a fine yellow dust that obscures the sun. Dominated by Muslim leaders, Kano is home to a virulent mistrust of the West and, at times, of the Nigerian central government in Abuja because of its emerging ties to the United States and Europe.

Prioritizing Treatment

"Polio, in Nigeria, is politics," says a doctor in Kano's main public hospital complex, who asked not to be named for fear of his job. The hospital was built by the British during colonial times in the 20s, and its long breezeways and white stone construction look like a set out of *The English Patient* or *Lawrence of Arabia*. "There's no getting around it. Everyone talks about [polio] eradication, but what we need is rehabilitation. Who talks about that? They'll never wipe out polio here; there's too many problems: political, cultural, bureaucratic. What can we do for the people who get the disease? No one is discussing this."

As we talk in the doorway to his office (he was too nervous talking to me to let me in to sit down), one toddler rocketed in from the hallway on his hands and knees, interrupting the doctor's comments; the child looked old enough to walk, except that his legs were noticeably thin and curled up behind him unnaturally, dragging uselessly on the floor. His harried mother soon dashed in and scooped him up to take him out of the office with apologies. The doctor locked eyes with me, his eyebrows raised, with an implied "see, this is what I'm saying" look.

Backlash Against the Vaccine

What brought us to this pass is this: Nigeria, long a polio hot spot, ended its polio vaccination program in 2003 in a colossally misguided protest of everything Western after the invasions of Afghanistan and, especially, Iraq. Religious leaders in Nigeria's predominantly Muslim north, twisting news reports about inadvertent contamination in some vaccinations, began preaching in mosques and market squares that polio vaccines were a Western plot to sterilize Muslim women, a plot by the same devious West that had just declared war on the Islamic world with its invasions of sovereign Muslim states.

And so, for 11 months in 2003 and 2004, polio vaccinations in northern Nigeria were suspended. Eleven months was all it took for the virus to not only gain a renewed foothold in Nigeria, but to spread to 10 other African nations that had previously wiped out the disease. WHO leaders feared a re-

Vaccine Fears and the 2005 Measles Outbreak

This outbreak of measles in the United States was caused by the importation of measles from abroad into a population of children whose parents objected to vaccination, primarily out of concern for adverse events related to the vaccine. Most patients were active young persons who had the potential to create hundreds of additional exposures in the two weeks before the Indiana State Department of Health was notified and efforts to contain the virus began. . . .

Refusing vaccination, rather than limited access to vaccination services, was a primary reason that many patients in the outbreak in Indiana were unvaccinated. Concern about adverse events, particularly related to media reports of a putative association between vaccinations and autism and of the dangers of thimerosal [a preservative], appeared to play a major role in the decision of these families to decline vaccination. Most families with these concerns continued to decline vaccination, even in the midst of an outbreak involving hospitalizations among their own community members. . . . In the United States, efforts to raise immunization rates have focused on improving preventive care for disadvantaged children, but different approaches may be necessary for populations such as this one, where belief systems, rather than access to health care, are the primary barrier to vaccination.

Amy Parker et al.,
New England Journal of Medicine, *August 3, 2006.*

newed global outbreak due to the suspensions, and undertook a lobbying campaign to restart the critical inoculations. They have now resumed, but in Kano it's too little, too late for far too many people.

Like Umar Ahmed, two years old. His father is an energetic and gregarious man named Aminu Ahmed, mostly healthy but with withered, useless legs after being struck with polio as a boy. But Aminu lives a full life; he's the informal head of the polio association in Kano and he is married and has seven kids, from age 20 to two. His oldest six children were immunized and are healthy, but his two-year-old, born during the immunization hiatus, has polio.

"This is Umar, my youngest boy," Aminu says, crawling over to his son, who can only crawl himself. "He's got the polio too. Poor son, poor son." But he laughs as he speaks and props up Umar with joy, coo-cooing him and trying to get a response. But Umar is remarkably quiet and dour for a two-year-old and merely totters in his father's grip.

Stemming the Spread of Disease

The tragedy of such scenes is made worse by considering how simple the actual administration of polio vaccine is. Two drops in the mouth from a small vial are all it takes to inoculate a child. Two simple drops in Umar's mouth 18 months ago would have spared him a lifetime of pain and difficulty.

Trying to make up for lost time, the World Health Organization conducted a massive countrywide inoculation campaign in Nigeria while I was there in April—an incredible 40 million inoculations in four hectic days nationwide, of every child in the country under five. I accompanied a vaccination team to a rural province to watch them work. Managing the group was Jibril Abdullahi, an official with the Nigerian National Programme for Immunization. He has spent years trudging through isolated outposts in northern Nigeria, figuring out ways to convince suspicious rural farmers that the vaccine is safe and does not affect fertility, which is the most common anti-vaccine rumor to echo out from Friday sermons at mosques.

"It is difficult to convince the rural people, sometimes," he says, making his way down a brown dirt path in the baking sun, his immaculate white robes flowing in a gentle breeze. "We do everything to convince the people that the vaccine is safe. We even take it ourselves"—he mimicked holding the dropper over his mouth—"and say, 'look, yes, it is safe.' Usually that helps, but you know what some women say? They say, 'you are old, you already have children, you can take it and it will not affect you.' And I say, oh my god."

He laughs sadly.

> *"The large number of internal refugees displaced by war and civil conflict creates ideal conditions for infectious diseases to spread."*

War Causes Disease Resurgence

Julie Hyland

Julie Hyland is a Central Committee member of the Socialist Equality Party in Britain. She is a full-time writer on political and social developments. The following viewpoint connects the 2007 outbreak of cholera in Iraq directly to the damage caused by war. Cholera is a highly contagious disease that is spread through contaminated water; the mass displacement of people fleeing war has stressed a sanitation infrastructure already heavily damaged. The easy transmission of this disease from person to person has already carried it across Iraq, where few hospitals remain to treat victims.

As you read, consider the following questions:

1. According to Hyland, how has available water contributed to the spread of cholera in Iraq?

Julie Hyland, "Cholera Outbreak in Northern Iraq," *World Socialist Web Site*, September 5, 2007. www.wsws.org. Reproduced by permission.

2. Why are refugees in particular at risk of contracting cholera, in the author's opinion?

3. Why can't hospitals adequately treat a sick population, according to Hyland?

Reports of a cholera outbreak in northern Iraq further highlight the social catastrophe facing millions in the country as a consequence of the US-led invasion and occupation.

Ten people have died and some 5,000 people have contracted the deadly water-borne disease due to lack of clean drinking water and poor sanitation.

In [early September, 2007], the World Health Organisation (WHO) said, "To date, it is estimated that Sulaimaniyah governorate experienced close to 5,000 cases since 10 August, with 10 deaths reported and 51 confirmed cases in Kirkuk."

The United Nations Children's Fund (UNICEF) reported at the same time, "Local authorities report that over 2,000 people have been affected so far by the outbreak, with five deaths reported and 500 patients admitted to hospital with severe diarrhoea within. . .two days alone."

Physician Dr. Burham Omar, who visited the area with representatives from Iraq's central health ministry, told [news agency] Al Jazeera that 2,250 people had been diagnosed in Sulaimaniyah and 2,000 in Kirkuk. A bacterial infection, cholera causes severe diarrhoea and vomiting and dangerous dehydration. Children and the elderly are particularly at risk.

No updated figures are available, but Dr. Dirar Iyad of Sulaimaniyah General Hospital said that he expects more deaths "over the next couple of days as victims are already in an advanced stage of illness."

A Dearth of Clean Water

The outbreak is particularly significant, given that northern Iraq is considered to be more stable than the rest of the country and has witnessed less fighting. But the social situation there is no less dire. More than half the population in Sulaimaniyah and Kirkuk does not have access to clean water. UNICEF reports that mains water [transported through pipes] is only available in Sulaimaniyah for two hours a day.

Zairyan Othman, health minister in the Kurdistan regional government, said, "Sulaimaniyah residents have been forced to rely on wells which I believe were exposed to sewage. . .due to cracked [pipes]."

Paolo Lembo, from the United Nations Development Programme, said, "The root cause of the outbreak lies in the inadequacy of the water supply system and deteriorated infrastructure."

Lembo, who had been visiting Jordan, warned, "The epidemic is expanding beyond its origin and spreading to other cities within Sulaimaniyah province and exhibiting a wider geographical coverage." Jordan is imposing visa requirements on Iraqis seeking to enter the country, while in Kuwait the Ministry of Health has announced "top level precautionary measures" against any possible infections being carried into the country.

Health officials later announced that they had traced the source of the outbreak in Sulaimaniyah to a water treatment plant. Test samples from the plant, which provides water to the entire province, had showed traces of the cholera bacteria.

Refugees Amid Destruction

More than a decade of sanctions, followed by US bombings and invasion, have destroyed much of Iraq's infrastructure, while the high civilian death toll, sectarian violence and displacement means there is a severe shortage of the skilled professionals necessary to carry out rebuilding.

In addition, the large number of internal refugees displaced by war and civil conflict creates ideal conditions for infectious diseases to spread. The UN High Commission for Refugees reported that the numbers of displaced persons had

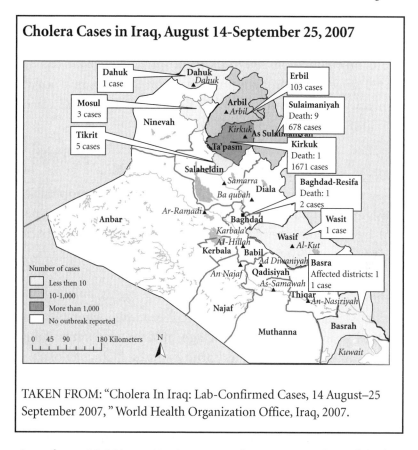

Cholera Cases in Iraq, August 14–September 25, 2007

Dahuk
1 case

Dahuk
Dahuk

Erbil
103 cases

Mosul
3 cases

Arbil
▲ *Arbil*

Ninevah

Sulaimaniyah
Death: 9
678 cases

Tikrit
5 cases

Kirkuk
As Sulaimaniyah
Ta'pasm

Kirkuk
Death: 1
1671 cases

Salaheldin

▲ *Samarra*
Ba qubah Diala
▲

Baghdad-Resifa
Death: 1
2 cases

Ar-Ramadi ▲

Anbar

Baghdad
Karbala'
Al-Hillah
Kerbala Babil
Wasif
Wasif
▲ *Al-Kut*

Wasit
1 case

Ad Diwaniyah Basra
An Najaf Qadisiyah
As-Samawah
Thiqar
▲ *An-Nasiriyah*

Basra
Affected districts: 1
1 case

Number of cases

- Less then 10
- 10–1,000
- More than 1,000
- No outbreak reported

Najaf

Muthanna

Basrah

Kuwait

0 45 90   180 Kilometers   N

TAKEN FROM: "Cholera In Iraq: Lab-Confirmed Cases, 14 August–25 September 2007," World Health Organization Office, Iraq, 2007.

risen from 50,000 to 60,000 a month. Many are forced to live in makeshift dwellings made out of refuse and are without access to clean water and the main sewerage system.

Dr. Juan Abdallah from Kurdistan's health ministry said the bad sanitation, particularly in refugee camps, had "put people at serious risk."

"The disease is spreading very fast," he said, pointing out that it was "the first outbreak of its kind here in the past few decades."

Cholera Was Predicted

Britain's *Independent* reported the situation facing 34-year-old Um Abir in Kirkuk, who said:

"My two children, husband and mother have been affected by cholera because we weren't able to get purified water and one of my children is very sick in hospital. We have been displaced since January [2007] and we have to camp near a rubbish tip which, according to the doctor, might be the reason for all of the family being affected."

There are now concerns that the outbreak could spread to Baghdad and the central province of Salahuddin.

Across Iraq, an estimated 70 percent of the population does not have adequate water supplies and less than 20 percent have effective sanitation. A lack of continuous electricity means that even where people are connected to the mains, water and sewerage cannot be pumped through properly. Iraq's main rivers, the Tigris and Euphrates, are highly polluted.

In March [2007], UN [United Nations] agencies had warned that the chronic shortage of drinking water would lead to an outbreak of waterborne diseases such as cholera in the summer months. UNICEF said that diarrhoea was already the second highest cause of child illness and death in Iraq, and that there had been an increase "even before the usual onset of the diarrhoea season in June," when the temperature can soar above 120 degrees Fahrenheit.

In June [2007], five cases of cholera were reported amongst children in Najaf, southern Iraq, in just three weeks.

Health Services Cannot Keep Up

A lack of medicine and healthcare is making it particularly difficult to control the disease. Doctors in northern Iraq have had to appeal for help, with UNICEF reporting that it has delivered 4,000 cannulae [tubes] and needles and 15,000 sachets of oral rehydration salts (ORS) necessary to prevent death from the dehydration induced by severe diarrhoea.

The collapse in Iraq's healthcare system is indicative of the destruction wreaked by US and British imperialism. During the 1980s Iraq's health system was regarded as amongst the best in the Middle East. Now it is virtually nonexistent.

The WHO has acknowledged, "Several wars and 13 years of economic sanctions left a heavy toll on the nutrition of the population, on the social structure, on the economy and on the health infrastructure and services.

"This is well depicted in the morbidity and mortality rates of the population of Iraq, particularly of infants, children and mothers."

Hospitals in Disrepair

According to the Iraq Medical Association (IMA), 90 percent of the 180 hospitals lack essential resources, while a health ministry spokesman said that "all hospital buildings and almost 90 percent of health centres require repair or total reconstruction."

But of a multimillion-dollar reconstruction plan announced by the US after the invasion for building 180 health clinics, only four had been finished and none opened by the end of 2005.

While billions in aid and reconstruction funds have gone missing, one doctor told health agencies, "Our hospitals look more like barns with lack of electric power, medicines, equipment and now doctors and surgeons because of the corrupt managers who care for nothing but filling their pockets with false contract money and conducting sectarian killings against doctors and patients."

In 2005, Medicine for Peace published its study of hospitals in Baghdad. This found that the majority "are generally unclean, unhygienic, and pose an imminent threat for hospital-acquired infections." Of the 13 hospitals, eight had no facilities to dispose of hazardous waste and 60 percent of the toilets did not work. Water was also reported to be unsafe to drink in at least four hospitals.

Essential medical equipment was also missing, or in short supply, including pain relief, sterile needles, masks, gloves and soaps. Seventy percent of the hospitals were unable to conduct the laboratory tests needed. There are reports of children dying of dehydration because hospital staff do not have the right needles to inject them with fluids.

In addition, the IMA reported that of the 34,000 Iraqi doctors registered prior to the invasion, over half had fled and at least 2,000 had been killed.

> *"Yellow fever and other related diseases could become more common as milder winters allow the seasonal survival of more mosquitoes."*

Climate Change Could Cause Disease Resurgence

James L. Dickerson

James L. Dickerson is a social worker turned journalist and book author; he has published more than twenty books and many more articles on health-related and other topics. The following viewpoint is excerpted from his book Yellow Fever, *an examination of the deadly, mosquito-borne disease in America. Practically forgotten today because of its prevention by public health programs, yellow fever appeared periodically throughout history killing thousands in epidemics. According to Dickerson, however, the disease has great potential to be a threat in the future if climate changes cause the earth to warm even a few degrees.*

As you read, consider the following questions:

1. According to Dickerson, what were Princeton and Cornell researchers surprised to learn about disease outbreaks and climate change?

2. Why are warmer temperatures more conducive to the spread of mosquitoes and disease pathogens, in the author's opinion?

3. What can West Nile virus tell researchers and health practitioners about yellow fever, according to Dickerson?

A 2002 study conducted by researchers at Princeton University and Cornell University concluded that climate warming is allowing disease-carrying viruses such as yellow fever to invade North America. As a result, the researchers warn that yellow fever and other related diseases could become more common as milder winters allow the seasonal survival of more mosquitoes. A warmer climate also could enable mosquitoes to move into areas once protected by cold weather. "In all the discussion about climate change, this has really been kind of left out," said Drew Harvell, a Cornell University marine ecologist and lead author of the study. "Just a one-or-two-degree change in temperature can lead to disease outbreaks."

An Alarming Increase of Disease

The comprehensive two-year study, developed by the National Center for Ecological Analysis and Synthesis, is the first to look at disease in terms of global warming. Said Harvell: "What is most surprising is the fact that climate sensitive outbreaks are happening with so many different types of pathogens—viruses, bacteria, fungi and parasites—as well as in such a wide range of hosts, including corals, oysters, terrestrial plants, birds and humans." Added coauthor Richard Ostfeld, from the Institute of Ecosystem Studies in Millbrook, New York: "This isn't just a question of coral bleaching for a few marine ecologists, nor just a question of malaria for a few health officials—the number of similar increases in disease incidence is astonishing. We don't want to be alarmist, but we are alarmed." Andrew Dobson, a Princeton epidemiologist associated with the study, says the risk for humans is going up: "The diseases we should be most worried about are the vector [insect] transmitted diseases." Even with small temperature increases, he concludes, natural ecosystems are disrupted in such a way as to create more fertile habitats for infectious diseases such a malaria and yellow fever.

Among those individuals not convinced that global warming will bring diseases such as yellow fever into the United States is the CDC's [Centers for Disease Control and Prevention's] Ned Hayes, which, according to one's point of view, is either comforting or highly disturbing. Hayes thinks that a yellow fever epidemic caused by global warming, as opposed to one caused by terrorists, has little chance of getting a foothold in the United States because of the country's high socioeconomic level and because of the prevalence of window screens and air conditioning. . . .

Not in agreement with Hayes are the researchers who conducted a 1998 study funded by the Climate Policy and Assessment Division of the EPA [Environmental Protection Agency], the National Institute of Public Health, and the Center for Medical, Agricultural, and Veterinary Entomology of the US Department of Agriculture. Using computers to simulate the circulation of the earth's climate, the researchers predicted that rising temperatures will increase the range of a mosquito that transmits the dengue fever virus. All three computer models used by the researchers indicated that dengue's epidemic potential increases with a relatively small temperature rise. At risk are the United States and all other countries around the world that are located in temperate zones, especially those that border on endemic areas where the disease is currently prevalent. "Since inhabitants of these border regions would lack immunity from past exposures, dengue fever transmission among these new populations could be extensive," says Jonathan Patz, lead author for the report and a physician at Johns Hopkins School of Public Health. "Our study makes

Memoir of Yellow Fever in 1793

I had scarcely become settled in Philadelphia when in July, 1793, the yellow fever broke out, and, spreading rapidly in August, obliged all the citizens who could remove to seek safety in the country. My father took his family to Bristol on the Delaware, and in the last of August I followed him. Having engaged in commerce, and having a ship at the wharf loading for Liverpool, I was compelled to return to the city on the 8th of September, and spend the 9th there. My business took me down to the Swedes' church and up Front street to Walnut street wharf, where I had my counting-house. Everything looked gloomy, and forty-five deaths were reported for the 9th. In the afternoon, when I was about returning to the country, I passed by the lodgings of the Vicomte de Noailles, who had fled from the Revolutionists of France. He was standing at the door, and calling to me, asked me what I was doing in town. "Fly," said he, "as soon as you can, for pestilence is all around us." And yet it was nothing then to what it became three or four weeks later, when from the first to the twelfth of October one thousand persons died. On the twelfth a smart frost came and checked its ravages.

Samuel Breck, Recollections of Samuel Breck, *1877.*

no claim that climate factors are the most important determinants of dengue fever. However, our computer models illustrate that climate change may have a substantial global impact on the spread of dengue fever."

Global Warming and Mosquitoes

Perhaps the best method of determining the effect of global warming on yellow fever is to examine the effect that warmer temperatures are having on related mosquito-borne diseases such as dengue, malaria, West Nile fever, and encephalitis. If they show signs of increased incidence, then it is only a matter of time before the yellow fever virus makes its reappearance.

Paul R. Epstein, associate director of the Center for Health and the Global Environment at Harvard, feels that those diseases are going to become more prevalent because of the mosquito's sensitivity to meteorological conditions. "Cold can be a friend to humans," he writes, "because it limits mosquitoes to seasons and regions where temperatures stay above certain minimums. Winter freezing kills many eggs, larvae and adults outright. . .within their survivable range of temperatures, mosquitoes proliferate faster and bite more as the air becomes warmer. At the same time, greater heat speeds the rate at which pathogens inside them reproduce and mature. . . .As whole areas heat up, then, mosquitoes could expand into formerly forbidden territories, bringing illness with them."

West Nile Virus

One of the most disturbing developments in recent years has been the arrival of the West Nile virus. In August 1999, tissue samples from a dead crow found in the New York City area and from a horse that died of a central nervous system disease on Long Island, New York, were sent to the National Veterinary Services Laboratories in Ames, Iowa, for identification. Meanwhile, more than two dozen cases of suspicious equine illness were identified in Suffolk and Nassau Counties on Long Island.

By September, the Centers for Disease Control and Prevention was able to identify the infected tissue samples as hosts to West Nile virus, a disease first isolated in 1937 in Africa and the Middle East. It is closely related to St. Louis encephalitis, which is indigenous to the United States and

Canada, but, as of August 1999, West Nile virus had never been isolated in tissue samples in North America.

Accompanying the deaths of dozens of horses and thousands of birds in the New York City area was an outbreak of human encephalitis that baffled health officials because it appeared to be a new strain. As the human death toll rose, genetic sequencing studies revealed that humans, birds, and horses were all infected by the same strain of West Nile, one that showed strong similarities to isolates from the Middle East.

Almost right away, the disease, which is spread from animals to humans by mosquitoes, began moving from New York to New Jersey and Connecticut, where eighty-three cases of West Nile were reported within one year. By 2005 the disease had spread all the way to California, infecting humans in almost every state except Maine, Alaska, and Hawaii. At greatest risk are those people over fifty years of age.

"Yellow fever is transmitted from human to mosquito to human, but with West Nile the reservoir of infection is the birds and possibly some reptiles and you have a different dynamic—humans are sort of incidental," says Dr. Ned Hayes. "You don't get human to human transmission with West Nile. The disease has spread east to west, north to south, going to both Canada and Mexico, but we still don't know what's going to happen in the United States. It is possible it could continue to cause locally intense epidemics in certain parts of the country, and it's also possible it might take a course like St. Louis encephalitis, which flares up after years of dormancy.". . .

Learning from Other Diseases

West Nile is of interest to yellow fever researchers because it demonstrates the speed with which a mosquito-induced disease can spread from state to state within a relatively brief period. Since West Nile can be spread only from animal to human, it is a friendlier disease, epidemically speaking, than yellow fever, which can spread with lightning speed from mosquito to human to mosquito to human. For those concerned about the reemergence of yellow fever in the United States, West Nile's unhindered march across the heartland offers little in the way of comfort.

Malaria is another mosquito-related disease that is raising red flags. Each year the disease kills more than three thousand people, mostly children. Some scientists predict that, by the end of [the twenty-first] century, the zone of malaria transmission will increase from one containing 45 percent of the world's population to one containing 60 percent. Malaria has a long history in the United States, but public health measures throughout the country were successful in isolating the disease and restricting it to California by the 1980s. As temperatures have risen since then, the threat has increased the incidence of malaria. In recent years, outbreaks have occurred in Florida, Texas, Georgia, Michigan, New Jersey, New York, and, to the surprise of many, Toronto, Canada.

Similarly, St. Louis encephalitis, a flavivirus related to Japanese encephalitis, has shown gains in recent years, with record spikes in the 1990s, which, incidentally, were the hottest years of this century. In the summer of 1999, New York City experienced an outbreak of encephalitis that killed a number of people. Normally, encephalitis, which causes inflammation of the brain, can effectively be treated, but the survival odds are lessened for those with weakened immune systems or for senior citizens.

At the time of the New York outbreak, Dr. Cathey Falvo, director for International and Public Health at New York Medical College, was concerned whether the increased temperatures would allow the disease to survive the winter. Falvo was particularly concerned about the effect that global warming was having on increased incidence of the disease. If global warming continues on its present course, she said, milder winters will result that will not be cold enough to kill the microbes, thus allowing the organisms to still be around when mosquitoes again become active in the spring.

"The Internet, while a wonderful tool for education information, can also be associated with disease transmission."

The Internet Could Be Used to Spark a Disease Epidemic

United Press International

The following viewpoint relates an example of how the Internet can contribute to an epidemic of disease. The San Francisco Department of Public Health stopped a potential syphilis outbreak by locating carriers of the disease in an AOL chat room where gay men would meet anonymously for sex. In cooperation with the Internet service provider and other organizations, authorities were able to identify the infected men. This case illustrates how the anonymity of the Internet can contribute to unsafe sex practices, which can, in turn, spread disease. United Press International is a news gathering organization based in Washington, D.C. that delivers headlines in top news, entertainment, health, business, science, and sports.

As you read, consider the following questions:

1. What did AOL allow Planet Out to do once they discovered the online meeting places?

2. According to the viewpoint, how are Internet chat rooms similar to bathhouses?

3. According to the viewpoint, the Internet can be associated with disease transmission. What else can it be used for?

G ay men cruising for anonymous sex on the Internet were spared a potentially deadly syphilis outbreak, thanks to a swift online response from the San Francisco Department of Health, according to researchers.

Internet Unleashes Syphilis Outbreak

The disease came to light when two men with syphilis revealed the source of their many sex partners to be an AOL chat room called SFM4M.

By teaming up with the Internet service provider [ISP] and a local marketing firm specializing in web access for gays, the Department of Public Health electronically identified five other men infected with the sexually transmitted disease [STD], and stopped what could have turned into an epidemic.

Dr. Jeffrey D. Klausner, who led the investigation, told UPI [United Press International] that his team's fast action gives a strong example of "what local health departments are doing with their syphilis elimination monies, that they are rapidly responding to outbreaks and doing good detective work to achieve the ultimate goal of syphilis elimination."

Klausner, director of STD Prevention and Control Services for the San Francisco Department of Public Health, added, "The Internet, while a wonderful tool for education information, can also be associated with disease transmission."

As soon as Klausner's team was made aware of this particular disease's presence in the area, and its online source, they contacted AOL and asked for the chat room patrons' contact information, a request that the ISP quickly denied to protect their customers' privacy.

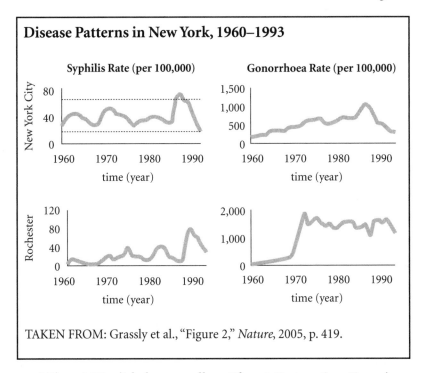

Disease Patterns in New York, 1960–1993

TAKEN FROM: Grassly et al., "Figure 2," *Nature*, 2005, p. 419.

What AOL did do was allow Planet Out, a San Francisco, California-based marketing firm with ties to the gay community, to contact these customers electronically and warn them of the syphilis-infested chatters using internet "handles" in lieu of real names.

Hundreds of men at risk in the online "meet" market were given lists of infected members and encouraged to seek diagnosis and treatment from the Department of Public Health if they even suspected exposure to the STD.

Klausner told UPI, "With this outbreak, we've recognized the importance of working with these online entities the same way that previously we would have worked with nightclubs or sex clubs or bars or bathhouses."

Using the Internet As Prevention

Michael Stalker, of the American Social Health Association in Research Triangle Park, N.C., an organization dedicated to ending STDs, told UPI that this sort of technological treatment is just what the doctor ordered.

"People are meeting in nontraditional ways and we're going to have to integrate this kind of outreach strategy into campaigns if we ever hope to have any impact on preventing and stopping STDs in the United States," says Stalker.

Anonymity Contributes to Syphilis Outbreak

Dr. Kathleen E. Toomey, director of the Division of Public Health, Georgia Department of Human Resources in Atlanta, Ga., told UPI, "The bottom line is that the Internet makes it so much easier for someone inclined to have anonymous sex or nearly anonymous sex."

Toomey, who also authored the editorial accompanying the study in this week's [July 2000] *Journal of the American Medical Association*, added, "I didn't see that what was going on in this outbreak was particularly unusual. I almost saw it as a virtual bathhouse."

Karen B. Martin, Program Coordinator for the Sexuality Center, North Shore-Long Island Jewish Health System in Lake Success, N.Y., told UPI, "It's terrifying."

"People are sexually active, they don't want to think about any consequence, and unless they get caught in some way they can go on. It's just that the volume increases if you have such an easy way of contacting people," says Martin.

Stalker told UPI that while ISPs can spread information on STDs until the cows come home, "the responsibility ultimately rests on the people who are engaging in sex."

"People need to know that syphilis is still out there, that it is still problematic, that if it's left undiagnosed and untreated it can lead to blindness, heart damage, and ultimately death," says Stalker, who encouraged those in search of more information to call the Center for Disease Control's National STD Hotline at 1-800-227-8922.

The study was funded by the San Francisco Department of Public Health in San Francisco, Calif.

Periodical Bibliography

The following articles have been selected to supplement the diverse views presented in this chapter.

Lisa W. Drew — "Combating the Lord of the Flies," *National Wildlife Magazine*, October/November, 2005.

Economist — "Still with Us: Two Pre-modern Ailments Are Making a Comeback," January 3, 2008.

Lea Berrang Ford — "Civil Conflict and Sleeping Sickness in Africa in General and Uganda in Particular," *Conflict and Health*, March 29, 2007. www.conflictand health.com.

William John Hoyt — "Anti-Vaccination Fever: The Shot Hurt Around the World," *Skeptical Inquirer*, January/February, 2004.

Melissa Knopper — "Calling the Shots: Parents Opting Out of Immunizations Raise Serious Public Health Issues," *E Magazine*, July/August, 2007. www.emagazine.com.

Maria Said — "The Chikungunya Question: What Effect Does Climate Change Have on the Spread of Disease?" *Slate*, February 6, 2008. www.slate.com.

Stephen Smith — "Hepatitis C Rises Among Young People: Mass. Officials Suspect Jump Tied to Drug Use," *Boston Globe*, May 8, 2007.

Doug Struck — "Climate Change Drives Disease to New Territory: Viruses Moving North to Areas Unprepared for Them, Experts Say," *Washington Post*, May 5, 2006.

University of North Carolina School of Medicine — "Resurgence and Spread of Syphilis in China Is a Rapidly Increasing Epidemic," *Science Daily*, January 12, 2007. www.sciencedaily.com.

OPPOSING
VIEWPOINTS®
SERIES

CHAPTER 2

How Should Society Respond to Resurgent Diseases?

Chapter Preface

B eing a member of a society is a continuous exercise in compromise. A well-balanced society allows neither complete freedom for the individual nor complete control by the group. Inevitably, someone will act in a way that upsets someone else. The degree to which this disharmony is tolerated varies among cultures, but many communities strike a balance between liberty and restriction that is acceptable to their citizens. In those balanced communities, people accept a certain degree of self-restraint for the greater benefits of belonging to a group with shared goals and privileges.

Disease adds an interesting spin to the problem of balance and wellness. Unfortunately, disease is often easily spread throughout a community, and one sick person can infect dozens, causing widespread discomfort and inconvenience at best, or even permanently harming or killing others. But is it a sick person's fault if others fall prey to the same illness? At what point can society "rightfully" intervene? At what point is a sick person responsible for the damage he or she does, if at all?

It is difficult to blame a sick person for infecting people when the symptoms of a disease have not yet manifested. One of the great tragedies of history is the death of millions of people in North and South America from diseases brought to them by European explorers—explorers who were not actually made sick by the diseases themselves. Smallpox is a prime example of this. European populations had suffered smallpox outbreaks for millennia; people who did not die from smallpox were naturally immune or had survived exposure. The sailors with Columbus and his successors carried the virus with them even though they were not made sick by it. The native peoples of North and South America had been isolated from Europe by two oceans and had not been exposed to the disease. When the virus arrived, they had no protection from it. While the European explorers and conquistadors went on to commit unspeakable atrocities against the native populations during the colonization of the Americas, this first deadly contact differs significantly from those intentional acts.

Epidemics that spread through communities of today suggest another aspect of culpability and infection: society's responsibility for failing to protect its members. If community leaders know about the presence of a deadly and infectious disease, do they have the right to violate the sufferer's privacy in order to warn others? Do they have the right to limit the freedom of disease victims until they are healed or dead if it means that no one else will get sick? Can the transmission of infection ever be rightly considered a crime? Lastly, is the protection of individual freedom the most important role society can play? It is important to consider whether the risk of contracting a disease from a member of the community is outweighed by the benefits of living in a community and the standards of living it makes possible.

The following chapter explores the responsibilities of community leaders and of community members, as well as the conflicts that can result when the general need to maintain public health interferes with individuals' rights and freedoms.

"A strain called USA300 has been a leading cause of MRSA infection . . . , and an exceptionally drug-resistant variant of it is now on the loose."

The Public Should Know about the Potential Risks of MRSA

Sabin Russell

Sabin Russell has been a journalist for thirty years. His stories cover public health issues such as bird flu, West Nile virus, mad cow, and other infectious diseases. In 2001, he was the recipient of the Science in Society Journalism Award from the National Association of Science Writers. In the following viewpoint, Russell describes the presence of a new strain of drug-resistant staphylococcus aureus (MRSA) infection—a "flesh-eating" bacterium—in the gay community of San Francisco. Because this disease can be transmitted through ordinary skin contact, the new strain can enter the larger population through casual social or business interactions.

As you read, consider the following questions:

1. Why are health workers concerned about this particular strain of MRSA, in Russell's opinion?

2. How many cases of MRSA occur in the United States each year, according to the author?

3. What is one way that Russell mentions that people can protect themselves from MRSA?

A new variety of staph bacteria, highly resistant to antibiotics and possibly transmitted by sexual contact, is spreading among gay men in San Francisco, Boston, New York and Los Angeles, researchers reported.

The study released online by the journal *Annals of Internal Medicine* found the highest concentrations of infection by the drug-resistant bug in and around San Francisco's Castro district and among patients who visit health clinics that treat HIV infections in gay men in San Francisco and Boston.

The culprit is a form of MRSA, or methicillin-resistant Staphylococcus aureus, a bug that was once confined to hospitalized patients but, since the late 1990s, has been circulating outside medical settings, afflicting anyone from injection-drug users to elementary school students. A strain called USA300 has been a leading cause of MRSA infection in this decade [2000–2009], and an exceptionally drug-resistant variant of it is now on the loose, researchers say.

MRSA in the Gay Community

The study estimated that 1 in 588 residents living within the Castro neighborhood 94114 ZIP code area is infected with that variant, which is resistant to six types of commonly used antibiotics. The risk of contracting this difficult-to-treat bug is 13 times greater for gay men than for the rest of the city's population, researchers found.

"We probably had it here first, and now it is spreading elsewhere," said Binh An Diep, a researcher at San Francisco

General Hospital and lead author of the report. "This is a national problem, and San Francisco is at the epicenter."

The germ typically causes boils and other skin and soft-tissue infections and, despite its resistance to some drugs, is still treatable by surgical drainage and several classes of antibiotics. What is unusual in this case is the high percentage of infections—up to 40 percent—occurring in the buttocks and genitalia.

Sexually Transmitted?

Although researchers have stopped short of declaring this form of staph a sexually transmitted disease, the infections are found where skin-to-skin contact occurs during sexual activity.

Most of the infections are limited to the skin surface, but the bacteria can invade deeper tissues or disseminate through the bloodstream. According to the federal Centers for Disease Control and Prevention, various forms of MRSA are causing 95,000 of these more costly and potentially life-threatening infections—and 19,000 deaths—annually in the United States.

Until [2007], staph infections had never been linked to sexual activity. Early [in 2007], New York City physicians traced three instances of staph infection apparently spread by sexual contact. Their report was published in February [2007], in the journal *Clinical Infectious Diseases*.

A month later, doctors from the Albany Medical Center in New York reported in the *Journal of Urology* three cases of multi-drug-resistant staph in the groins of three patients—one of whom developed a form of rapid-tissue destruction popularly known as "flesh-eating bacteria" disease. The patients recovered after treatments with surgery and antibiotics.

An Aggressive Strain

San Francisco General Hospital physicians have been battling an aggressive strain of MRSA, called USA300, since 2001. The most recent study estimates that this strain alone is infecting about 2,000 city residents a year.

Maggot Therapy vs. MRSA

The first study we did was an observational treatment of consecutive patients with MRSA colonised wounds with larvae therapy. We apply about 100 sterile larvae of the greenbottle fly to the wound, these stay on for about 3–5 days, they go on the size of a small grain of rice and they come off about ten times larger, the sort of maggot you could use for fishing tackle. We used about three to five applications of these and of thirteen consecutive patients, twelve were completely cleared out of the MRSA. . . .

It does appear that the maggot is a bit like a magnet if you imagine the MRSA as iron filings, it appears to be attracted to the cuticle. We're also dissecting out larvae removed from wounds to see if they ingest them and we're looking at a number of possibilities to see if the substances they secrete, for example, kill off or at least stop reproduction of the bacteria.

Andrew Bouton, TheNakedScientists.com, May 2007.

But the latest problem is being caused by a new variant of USA300 that was first detected in a San Francisco patient in 2003. Among the six antibiotics it is resistant to are three that are normally considered for treatment of suspected MRSA. The study estimated that 200 cases of this highly drug-resistant variant are turning up in San Francisco each year, mostly among gay men.

"We are nowhere near the peak," Diep said. "The peak will occur when it spreads into the general population."

Diep said there is reason to believe that the more drug-resistant strain will make that leap because it is just a slight variant of USA300, which became one of the most common strains of MRSA in the United States only a few years after it was first detected.

Theories about Susceptibility

The latest study focuses on the spread of the more drug-resistant strain in San Francisco and Boston, but reports of the bug are turning up in New York and Los Angeles.

Just why the new, more drug-resistant variety is concentrated among gay men is not yet known. Patients infected with HIV appear to run a higher risk of infection, but the study suggests that gay men are being infected with the staph germ regardless of whether they are HIV-positive.

One factor that could be in play is a medical history of heavy use of antibiotics, which creates conditions for breeding drug-resistant strains. Any patient, HIV-positive or not, who has had high previous exposure to antibiotics might be more susceptible.

On a Personal Level

The good news is that, once the public is aware of the risk, there are ways to prevent the spread of drug-resistant staph. It can be as simple as soap and water.

"Taking a shower after sexual contact may minimize contamination," said Dr. Chip Chambers, director of infectious diseases at San Francisco General, a co-author of the study. "Ordinary soap will do. It dilutes the concentration of bacteria. You don't need antibacterial soap."

Chambers stressed that some people, no matter how fastidious, could be more prone than others to staph infections. They could have unknown genetic traits or a history of antibiotic use that raises the risk.

"Despite one's best efforts, it is still possible, of course, to get a staph infection," he said. "This is why if one has a cut or open wound that it is important to clean it out and keep it clean."

Still Treatable

The new variant of USA300 is resistant to the antibiotics erythromycin, clindamycin, tetracycline, Cipro-like antibiotics and drugs in the penicillin family. It also does not respond to mupirocin—a gel that is often used to kill MRSA growing in people's noses.

That still leaves a variety of antibiotics that will kill the new USA300 strain, but they tend to be more expensive and require intravenous drips. One common oral antibiotic, Bactrim, is still effective against it.

Chambers also pointed out that researchers at San Francisco General have shown that many skin sores and boils caused even by these drug-resistant strains of staph often can be treated without any antibiotics, just by surgical drainage of pus.

One of the paradoxes of bacterial infections is that using antibiotics to treat them is one of the quickest ways to promote antibiotic resistance. Although the drugs sometimes are essential, overuse is weakening their effectiveness worldwide.

"All it took was for one irresponsible, publicity-seeking researcher in San Francisco to hype an outbreak . . . , and suddenly we find a simultaneous outbreak of. . . hysterics."

The Hysteria Over MRSA Is Unfounded

Jim Burroway

Jim Burroway is the editor of Box Turtle Bulletin, *an online publication that debunks stereotypes and corrects misinformation about the gay community. In the following viewpoint, Burroway issues a direct response to the media hysteria prompted by study findings that claimed that a strain of drug-resistant bacteria, known as MRSA, was running rampant among gays in San Francisco. The author argues that the researchers sensationalized their findings in order to draw attention to their work; he also argues that gays caught the MRSA bacteria because they are part of the "general" population, not because it originated among them.*

Jim Burroway, "Is MRSA the New Gay Plague?" *Box Turtle Bulletin*, January 19, 2008. www.boxturtlebulletin.com. Reproduced by permission.

As you read, consider the following questions:

1. Rather than gay people, what group has been identified by the Centers for Disease Control and Prevention as having a high risk for contracting MRSA, according to Burroway?

2. As reported by the author, what percentage represents the prevalence of MRSA in the Castro neighborhood of San Francisco?

3. What parallels does Burroway find between the media's coverage of the AIDS epidemic in the 1980s and the coverage of MRSA in 2008?

A new study came out [in January 2008] from researchers at the University of California, San Francisco [UCSF], which found a high rate of drug-resistant staph infection among "men who have sex with men" in San Francisco and Boston. This staph infection, known as methicillin-resistant *Staphylococcus aureus* (MRSA) is a bacteria that is resistant to certain antibiotics. There are essentially two classes of MRSA: healthcare-associated MRSA which has plagued hospitals and other medical facilities, and community-associated MRSA (CA-MRSA) which is found outside of healthcare settings. This latest study from UCSF examines an outbreak of a particular form (USA300) of CA-MRSA in the Castro district of San Francisco and among gay men in Boston.

With this latest study, MRSA quickly became the newest "gay plague" and lead author Binh Diep rang alarm bells around the world. . . .

Not a Gay Disease

According to the medical literature—which Diep ought to be well acquainted with—the USA300 variant of MRSA is already widespread in the general population. And gay men, who *are* in the general population, had little to do with it. If the medical literature is any indication, it's the "general population" that's responsible for spreading MRSA into the gay community.

Over the past decade, community-associated MRSA (mostly USA300) has been reported in Atlanta, Albany, Baltimore, Birmingham, Boston, Chicago, Detroit, El Paso, Houston, Las Cruces (NM), Los Angeles, Memphis, Minneapolis, New York, Oakland, and Sacramento, as well as in the states of Florida, Hawaii, Kentucky, Indiana, Minnesota, North Dakota, Tennessee, and Washington. (This list is *not* complete, by the way). CA-MRSA has infected inmates in jails and prisons and children in day care, as well as American Indians on reservations, rural residents of Southwestern Alaska, and Pacific Islanders of Hawaii.

Internationally, dangerous forms of MRSA have been reported in Australia, Canada, Denmark, France, Germany, Ireland, Japan, the Netherlands (where one study showed how it can be transmitted in families), New Zealand, Norway, Portugal, South Korea, Spain, Sweden, Switzerland, Taiwan, United Kingdom, Uruguay, and Western Samoa. Again, this is not a complete list by any means.

All of these outbreaks were among the "general population" and not one was blamed on gay men.

The Athletic Menace?

But a review of the literature shows that one could make a case for blaming athletes. In 1998, the *Archives of Internal Medicine* reported on an outbreak which struck nearly a quarter of the members of a high school wrestling team in southern Vermont, who then passed the infection on to others in the surrounding community. But unlike Dr. Diep, the good doctors who wrote that report didn't provide any dark warnings that if the epidemic spread from those disease-laden wrestlers to the general population, it would be "unstoppable."

Maybe they should have. Since then we've seen outbreak clusters among high school wrestlers in Indiana, fencing club members in Colorado, college football players in Los Angeles and Pennsylvania, high school football players in Illinois and Texas, and rugby players in Britain. In 2004, one in ten football players at a college in the Northeast were infected. "Cosmetic body shaving and turf burns" were cited as contributing factors. In 2006, the *Journal of Athletic Training* reported on a 2003 outbreak affecting nearly 16% of the USC [University of Southern California] Trojans football team.

MRSA has also struck professional football, landing Miami Dolphins Junior Seau and Charlie Rogers in the hospital in 2003 and sidelining Washington Redskins' Brandon Noble in 2006. Dr. Holly J. Benjamin, writing for the *Clinical Journal of Sports Medicine*, has described MRSA as "the latest sports epidemic." The problem has gotten to be so widespread that the CDC [Centers for Disease Control and Prevention] has published prevention measures written especially for athletes. . . .

Scapegoating Gay People

But instead of panicking over the athletic menace, the media all over the world is fixated over the latest gay plague. The *Toronto Star* falsely asserted that this latest study "discover[ed] a new strain" of a super-bug "hitting gay men." Headlines in Britain screamed, "Flesh-eating bug strikes San Francisco's gay community," while Australians panicked over the more widespread, "Flesh-eating bug spreads among gays."

What is it about gay men that sets everyone into fits of terror?

MRSA Is Everywhere

When the journal *Clinical Infectious Diseases* reported on the heterosexual transmission of MRSA in New York, nobody worried about a super-bug hitting straight men and women.

When the CDC reported in 2004 of an outbreak among 1.1% of naval recruits in the Southeastern U.S. and *Clinical*

Pro Football vs. MRSA

[In] two years, the [Washington] Redskins have had five cases of MRSA, team physician Tony Casolaro said. . . .

In addition to spending $17,000 on a new Jacuzzi system that is equipped with an ultraviolet light filtering system designed to kill germs, the Redskins hired SportsCoatings Inc. to treat the training room, locker rooms and weight rooms with an anti-microbial coating the company claims will help kill various strains of the bacteria. . . .

In 2003, Jeffrey Hageman, an epidemiologist with the CDC and expert in sports-related MRSA cases, investigated the St. Louis Rams and found that five of 58 players developed MRSA infections, likely from turf abrasions. In his research on the Rams, Hageman found linebackers, linemen and players of high body mass to be particularly susceptible.

Howard Bryant, Washington Post, *August 3, 2006.*

Infectious Diseases reported a 3% prevalence among US army trainees at Brooke Army Medical Center, there were no warnings of a super-bug infecting the military. And when *Military Medicine* reported an outbreak on a naval ship at sea or when the *Journal of Clinical Microbiology* reported that 11% of naval trainees in San Diego had MRSA during the summer of 2002, there was no seaman scare.

When the *New England Journal of Medicine* reported in 2005 that 9% of the St. Louis Rams football team had MRSA during the 2003 football season, there was no hue and cry over a flesh-eating jock staph.

When *Epidemiology and Infections* reported on a September 2004 outbreak which infected 14% of a communal religious community in upstate New York, there were no demands to halt the promotion of religion as an acceptable lifestyle.

But when the *Annals of Internal Medicine* reported that the prevalence of MRSA in the Castro's 94114 zip code reached a tiny smidgen of *0.17%*, all hell broke loose. And guess what? Buried deep within that dry academic report—the report that few reporters ever bothered to read—was this: the margin of error was a whopping $+/- 0.13\%$. Also buried was a warning that these findings are not generalizable to gay men everywhere, and that nothing in the study points to specific sexual behaviors as risk factors. In fact, MRSA is easily transmitted by ordinary skin-to-skin contact, as well as contact with contaminated surfaces. . . .

Shades of AIDS

So what gives? Where did the media get the idea that a brand new, giant super-bug was eating San Francisco?

Well, much of the blame can be laid squarely at Dr. Diep's own publicity stunt. It was his sensationalist comments in his press release—written precisely to grab journalists' attention—that started the panic in the first place. And that panic was fueled even further by his alarmist statements to reporters from Reuters and the *San Francisco Chronicle*. . . .

It is shades of the 1980s all over again. Anti-gay demagogues were eager to politicize AIDS when they found that it was a useful weapon against the LGBT [lesbian, gay, bisexual, and transgendered] community. Today we see a new generation of demagogues politicizing MRSA in much the same way. And all it took was for one irresponsible, publicity-seeking researcher in San Francisco to hype an outbreak in the Castro, and suddenly we find a simultaneous outbreak of anti-gay hysterics everywhere else.

A Few Lessons

The good news is that better judgment is prevailing at the CDC. They are now trying to counter the anti-gay hysteria and undo some of the damage from Diep's sensationalist comments. Two days after the news hit the papers, the CDC released a statement saying:

> The strains of MRSA described in the recent *Annals of Internal Medicine* have mostly been identified in certain groups of men who have sex with men (MSM), but have also been found in some persons who are not MSM. It is important to note that the groups of MSM in which these isolates have been described are not representative of all MSM, so conclusions can not be drawn about the prevalence of these strains among all MSM. . . .
>
> MRSA is typically transmitted through skin-to-skin contact, which occurs during a variety of activities, including sex. There is no evidence at this time to suggest that MRSA is a sexually transmitted infection in the classical sense.

MRSA is dangerous if left untreated, and while it is resistant to some forms of antibiotics, it's not resistant to all forms. In some cases, the wound might have to be lanced and drained. Only very rarely is surgery required.

And the best news is that MRSA is easily preventable. Cover any cuts, scrapes or sores, and wash your hands and shower regularly—ordinary soap and water does the trick. And don't share personal items—toothbrushes, razor blades, sheets and towels, and so forth. Preventing its spread is just that easy.

It's time we all took a deep breath, calmed down, and learned a few lessons from all this. MRSA is not new, and gays aren't spreading a new and deadly disease into the "general population." It's already been there for decades. If anything, all the evidence indicates that the "general population" has spread MRSA into the Castro and other places.

> *"The state certainly has a duty to pro-
> tect the public from extreme health
> risks, but it needs to do it in a careful,
> scientific and humane way."*

Individual Rights Should Not Be Disregarded in the Interests of Public Health

Robert Daniels et al., interviewed by Amy Goodman

Amy Goodman is the host and executive producer of Democracy
Now!, *an independent daily news program airing on more than
650 TV and radio stations in North America. She is also the author of a weekly syndicated column that won the 2007 James
Aronson Award for Social Justice Reporting. The following viewpoint is an interview with several people who know Robert
Daniels, an American who was imprisoned for a little over a
year in extreme solitary confinement for exposing people in public to a deadly strain of drug-resistant tuberculosis. Daniels
claims he was unaware of the danger of the health risk to others
and that his rights have been violated.*

Robert Daniels et al., interviewed by Amy Goodman, "Is Sickness a Crime? Arizona
Man with TB Locked Up Indefinitely in Solitary Confinement," *Democracy Now!*, April
6, 2007. www.democracynow.org. Reproduced by permission.

As you read, consider the following questions:

1. What action did Robert Daniels commit that resulted in his incarceration, according to Goodman?

2. Is Daniels's isolation being dictated by medical personnel or by law enforcement officials, according to the viewpoint?

3. Who, according to the viewpoint, is most at risk to catch tuberculosis?

A*my Goodman*: Is sickness a crime? We turn now to the case of an Arizona man who's been jailed without committing a single crime. 27-year-old Robert Daniels is being held against his will in a Phoenix hospital ward reserved for sick prisoners. If state officials have their way, he could be there for the rest of his life. Daniels is suffering from a deadly strain of tuberculosis [TB] known as XDR-TB. Doctors say he's virtually untreatable.

Daniels contracted the disease while living in Russia. He returned to the United States, agreed to a voluntary quarantine in residential care. But Daniels violated his agreement when he went outside without a mask. Daniels says he misunderstood how much of a health risk he posed, in part because he hadn't been forced to wear a mask in Russia.

Today, Daniels has been forced to live in a hospital cell in complete isolation. His only visitors are medical staff. Sheriff's deputies have taken away his television, his radio, his phone and his computer. He's under 24-hour surveillance. The light in his room is never turned off, even at night. His only contact with the outside world is a pay phone.

Worse than Prison

Daniels recently described his ordeal in a phone interview with the Arizona radio station KJZZ.

Robert Daniels: I never thought that this could happen. I'm telling you, I'm sometimes sitting on a bed, and I'm just crying because of all the quietness. I don't have, you know, a permission to take a normal shower, and I have to spit wash. It's really cold, especially at this time. I can't, you know, even—I can't even spit wash normally.

They're telling me I'm an inmate. They gave me a booking number, you know, which is for what? For having TB? Booking number? It's just being all ridiculous. If they want me to be isolated, that's fine with me, but, you know, they don't have the right to isolate me from the other world, especially my family, especially from the media, the news, the everything. I mean, I'm all alone here. I don't even know what the hell is going on in the world. I'm not being isolated. I'm being incarcerated, and I have nobody to talk to. My mental health is going down. I'm just slowly dying.

Goodman: Robert Daniels is speaking to the Arizona radio station KJZZ. [Recently,] *Democracy Now!* spoke to a former worker at the Maricopa County Medical Center who has kept in touch with Daniels. She spoke to us on condition that she not be identified and that we disguise her voice.

Former Maricopa County Medical Center Worker: He says he cries a lot, says he's very depressed. You have to understand that he is in what, for all practical purposes, is in solitary confinement. He is in a room in the hospital that, number one, has no hot water, has no privacy, has no natural lights. The windows are blocked.

He has no visitation. He can make calls, but who can afford to accept their collect calls? At 4:00, they turn the telephone on. He doesn't really have magazines. If he does, it's rare. He doesn't have TV. He does not have a radio. So all he has is the quietness of the room and then the nurses coming in when they bring him his medicine.

He cannot take a shower. There are no showers right now. There are no showers on the floor. But he has not had a shower since January. So he gets nothing for personal hygiene other than a basin of water and some, you know, washcloths.

Tuberculosis Patient Has Lung Removed

Mr. Daniels arrived at National Jewish [Medical and Research Center] on July 17 [2007]. He underwent surgery July 31 at the University of Colorado Hospital to remove his entire left lung, which was extensively damaged and infected with tuberculosis. He has been recovering since then at National Jewish while his physicians worked to get him on a regimen of antibiotics that is effective but has minimal side effects.

"I am cautiously optimistic about Robert's chances for recovery," said Dr. Huitt.

Editor's note: Daniels returned to Russia in 2007, after this procedure.

William Allstetter, www.nationaljewish.org, September 18, 2007.

So he's unable to shampoo his hair, because the faucet in a detention unit is very small, and, of course, with no warm water in there, he can't shampoo anyway.

Goodman: That was a former worker at the Maricopa County Medical Center, speaking about the tuberculosis patient, Robert Daniels. We also spoke with Daniels's wife, Alla Danielova. She lives in Moscow in Russia with their son, five-year-old Dmitry. Alla has not seen her husband in over a year.

Alla Danielova: I would like the government to give him a room without guards, without handcuffs or chains, because he's not a criminal.

Public Safety Taken Too Far

Goodman: Robert Daniels's harsh incarceration has sparked a controversial debate over whether Arizona officials have gone too far in the name of public safety. Dan Pochoda is legal director for the American Civil Liberties Union [ACLU] in Arizona, considering taking up Daniels's case. Dan joins us on the phone from Phoenix. And we're also joined by Lawrence Gostin, director of the Center for Law and the Public's Health at Johns Hopkins and Georgetown Universities. On the line with us from Boston is George Annas, a professor of health law at Boston University's School of Public Health.

I want to begin with Dan Pochoda. Just tell us further what's happening right now and why Robert Daniels is in jail.

Dan Pochoda: Well, as you mentioned, he is in jail because of an initial decision by the county health officials, that he required to be quarantined and have his liberty taken away. We are not in a position to assess whether that the reasons that underlay that decision made sense in the first instance, but it is clear to us that the conditions that he is being held under— and I do mean "held"—are not medically dictated, but rather dictated by the sheriff, and that despite clear court cases, he's being held in an unconstitutional and punitive manner much worse than other persons in the hospital, even persons who have to be isolated and, as admitted by the Sheriff's Department, like any other jail inmate. He is not a jail inmate, and he will be facing these conditions for many years to come, and they are clearly impacting his mental and physical well-being.

Goodman: Professor Gostin, can you respond to this situation?

Lawrence Gostin: Well, I actually think that was stated quite well. And there's no question that if somebody has extremely drug-resistant tuberculosis, that if it's transmitted to others, it can be very dangerous, because the form of infection that you transmit to the other person is similarly very resistant, if not impossible, to treat. And so, what you'd be doing is causing really serious harm. And so, I think that public health authorities are justified in trying to prevent that, but it needs to be the least restrictive alternative, for the shortest amount of time, and in decent and humane conditions. Courts have stated that this is not a punitive decision. It shouldn't be. It should be driven by public health and medical authorities, not by police or other corrections officials. And so, in short, the state certainly has a duty to protect the public from extreme health risks, but it needs to do it in a careful, scientific and humane way.

Goodman: Professor George Annas of Boston University, what do you think should happen here? Does this case of Robert Daniels surprise you?

George Annas: Well, it disturbs me more than it surprises me. It's not surprising that when we get the public basically totally ignorant of infectious, contagious diseases, then they're told there's a new disease here that could kill you and it's not treatable, what do you expect? How do you expect people to react, especially people in law enforcement? They're going to react, to use the tools they have. And the tools they have are jails and punishment. And Professor Gostin is right: that's wrong. We shouldn't be doing that.

We do not want this disease in the United States, although it's clearly here. And we do want to take reasonable measures to make sure that it's not spread in the community. But it does not require locking anybody up in a jail. TB is not that easy to get. I mean, if you hang around in homeless shelters, in prisons or in places where a lot of people are immuno-compromised, like have HIV disease, then it's certainly going to be spread. But just someone walking around, at least if he doesn't go right up next to you and breathe in your mouth for a couple of hours, you're not going to get TB that way. So we have to learn something about tuberculosis, as well as something about the inappropriateness and, I think, unconstitutionality of locking people up with the disease.

Goodman: Professor Gostin, what kind of rights does Robert Daniels have right now? What can he do?

Gostin: Well, Professor Annas did state it correctly and wisely. There is a constitutional right to humane treatment.

The courts have basically said that when there's a civil confinement, whether it's the mentally ill or for reasons of infectious diseases, it needs to be necessary for the public's health, and it is absolutely correct that TB is not as easily transmissible as the public believes, but it can be transmitted. And when that happens, there needs to be humane conditions. It can't be punitive; it can't be in correctional or prison kinds of environments. So you need to give somebody basic, decent humane care and treatment. It doesn't sound at all like that's the case here, and I would have thought that the courts would be very sympathetic to this. My judgment is that the courts would uphold only the minimal necessary to confine him for the sake of the public, but would not allow an indefinite confinement the way they're proposing, and certainly not in the conditions they're proposing.

Goodman: Professor Gostin, can you explain what tuberculosis is? What about the outbreak of the 1990s here in New York City? New York forced TB patients into detention in that outbreak.

Gostin: Yeah, I mean, it's—TB is a bacterial infection. It's very prevalent throughout world. In fact, one out of every three or four people have tuberculosis infection, but don't get the disease. So only a small number of those will go on to get the disease. It's prevalent in other parts of the world. It exists in the United States. And in the 1990s in New York and a number of other cities, there was a rise of cases of what they called multidrug-resistant tuberculosis. And more recently, not in the United States particularly, but in other countries, like Russia and South Africa and other places, there's been something called extremely drug-resistant tuberculosis, which means that it really can't even be treated with second- and third-line medications. And that's what I gather we're talking about here, something that is extremely resistant to treatment. And the reason is, is that the bacteria just simply adapt to the medications and become resistant and resist them.

Goodman: So, we're talking about a man who's been in prison now for almost, what a year—nine, ten months. . . . Dan Pochoda, what are the ACLU's plans now in Arizona? Are you going to take up Robert Daniels's case?

Pochoda: We are, as the situation has changed over the months. He was initially confined, as was stated, by a civil proceeding in the Arizona state courts, that was brought by the Maricopa County Health Department. And things were OK, in terms of the conditions, for a while. It was a decision by the Maricopa County Health Department to turn over the body, so to speak, and control of the decisions of most of the routines of Mr. Daniels to the Maricopa County Sheriff's Department. And the Sheriff's Department, predictably, has stated, "We will treat this person in our jail ward as any other jail inmate." And flowing from that is the deprivations of loss of things like a TV set and hot water and a computer and any type of music player, light on in his cell, because—things that would be allowed any other patient, no less a patient that has to stay in a room. And no one is disputing the need for a locked room here.

We have recently been in touch with the attorney for Mr. Daniels, who was appointed on the initial underlying decision, and we will be working with him to change, at a minimum, the conditions of confinement. As has been stated, it's cruelly unconstitutional to hold someone who is civilly committed in this punitive manner. Nothing could be more punitive than the stark conditions facing Mr. Daniels. If necessary, it would be constitutional litigation that we would be involved in.

> "Courts have upheld the exercise of compulsory detention powers for public health purposes."

Individual Rights Must Sometimes Bow to Public Health Interests

David P. Fidler, Lawrence O. Gostin, and Howard Markel

David P. Fidler is an expert on international law and public health and a professor at the Indiana University School of Law; Lawrence O. Gostin is a professor of global health law at Georgetown University; and Howard Markel is a professor of communicable diseases at the University of Michigan. The following viewpoint is a response to the global public health and legal issues that arose in 2007 when Andrew Speaker, a man already diagnosed with drug-resistant tuberculosis, traveled from the United States to Europe and back again. The authors argue that sometimes limiting personal freedoms to protect the public from drug-resistant, contagious diseases is justified.

David P. Fidler, Lawrence O. Gostin, and Howard Markel, "Through the Quarantine Looking Glass: Drug-Resistant Tuberculosis and Public Health Governance, Law, and Ethics," *Journal of Law, Medicine & Ethics*, vol. 35, no. 4, Winter 2007, pp. 616–624. Reproduced by permission.

As you read, consider the following questions:

1. What conditions first prompted the cooperation of international groups to control public health, according to the authors?

2. In the authors' opinion, what is the difference between quarantine and isolation from a public health standpoint?

3. How do the authors justify the compulsory isolation of Andrew Speaker, the man with tuberculosis who ignored instructions not to travel?

The idea that involuntary detention for public health purposes reflects political and social phenomena beyond breaking the chain of pathogen transmission is, of course, not new. One common response to epidemics, across time and national boundaries, has been the use of individual and group control measures. If we look at isolation and quarantine actions as part of the progression of an epidemic, we can detect impulses that often help shape it. These include the following: (1) avoiding the ill, or those perceived to be ill, particularly if the disease is thought to be contagious; (2) negotiations over how experts and the community at large understand the disease, especially in terms of cause, prevention, and amelioration; (3) the complex political, economic, and social battles that guide or obstruct a community's efforts to respond to the epidemic; and (4) the extent to which ethnicity and perceptions about a social group associated with a disease frame the responses that shape control measures aimed at individuals or communities.

Many societies have responded to visitations of contagious diseases by avoiding and isolating the ill. The Old Testament records involuntary detention and social distancing and their corresponding sanitary procedures, including the use of the ram's horn, or shofar, traditionally sounded during the Jewish High Holidays, to signal a case of diphtheria or other contagious disease in the community. In ancient Greece, the writings of Thucydides (c.460–c.400 BC) and Hippocrates (c.460–c.370 BC) demonstrated that Greek societies attempted to avoid contact with the contagious. The Roman authority on medicine, Galen of Pergamon, warned that specific diseases made it "dangerous to associate with those afflicted." In AD 549, the Byzantine emperor Justinian enacted one of the first laws requiring restraint and isolation of travelers from regions where the plague was known to be raging. Similar forms of detention for plague directed against sailors and foreign travelers were also practiced in seventh-century China and other parts of Asia and Europe during the Middle Ages. Not surprisingly, these quarantine actions recognized the relationship between epidemic disease transmission and human movement and migration.

The word *quarantine* originates from the Italian words *quarantenara* and *quaranta giorni*, which referred to the 40-day period during which Venice isolated ships before their goods, crew, and passengers could disembark during the plague-ridden days of the 14th and 15th centuries. In about 1374, Venice enacted its 40-day quarantine regulation, and, in 1403, the municipality established the first maritime quarantine station, or lazaretto, on the island of Santa Maria di Nazareth. From medieval times on, shutting the gates of a city or port to those suspected of being ill, and isolating sick people within, represented the best, and often the only, means for stemming an epidemic.

The growth of international commerce and travel during the Renaissance and the subsequent three centuries contributed to the spread of infectious diseases around the globe. To prevent the entry of contagion, sanitary cordons (literally a ring of armed soldiers guarding against entry of diseased persons) and quarantines were used in France, Britain, Austria, Germany, Russia, and other European and Asian nations from the 14th through 19th centuries. By the mid-1800s, in response to devastating cholera and plague epidemics imported into Europe from Turkey and Egypt, and the economic burdens created by different national quarantine systems, European nations with the strongest commercial or colonial interests began to engage in international cooperation. These efforts included attempts to harmonize quarantine policies, a process aided by the emergence of the germ theory of disease in the late 19th century. Commencing in 1851, these International Sanitary Conferences continued well into the 20th century, generated the first uses of international law for public health purposes, and led to the creation of the first international health organizations. . . .

Quarantine and Public Health Laws

The manner in which quarantine powers have been intertwined with religious, political, economic, and social practices, interests, values, and prejudices makes quarantine authority an important governance topic. Isolation and quarantine involve the compulsory application of public authority to individuals or groups and, thus, these acts create tensions between protecting population health and respecting individual autonomy and dignity. These tensions stimulate the heightened interest isolation and quarantine trigger. Principles in public health law and ethics shape the governance task of managing those tensions, and these principles provide insight into how societies organize and perceive the use of the power to implement isolation and quarantine measures.

From a governance perspective, delineation of the different facets of a government's quarantine powers is important legally and ethically. These powers encompass the authority to detain persons involuntarily for public health purposes. Although isolation and quarantine are often used interchangeably, they are not the same. Quarantine involves the restriction of the movement of persons who have been exposed, or potentially exposed, to infectious disease, during the period of communicability, to prevent transmission of infection during the incubation period. Quarantine seeks to prevent the spread of dangerous, highly contagious pathogens, such as smallpox, plague, and Ebola fever, particularly if medical countermeasures are ineffective or unavailable.

Isolation involves separating, for the period of communicability, *known* infected persons from the community so as to prevent or limit the transmission of the infectious agent. Modern science and medicine can usually detect whether a person has an infectious condition. Accordingly, isolation often is the action taken rather than quarantine, and this outcome is particularly true for TB [tuberculosis]. Isolation is, where possible, linked to treatment, including directly observed therapy (DOT) for TB, which the detaining authority offers to, or imposes on, persons subject to isolation orders.

Quarantine and Judicial Practices

Public health authorities possess a variety of powers to restrict the autonomy or liberty of persons who pose a public health threat because they are infected with, or have been exposed to, dangerous, contagious pathogens. These authorities can direct individuals to discontinue risk behaviors (e.g., "cease and desist" orders), compel them to submit to physical examination or treatment, and detain them using public health or criminal justice powers. . . .

The Constitution does not mention isolation or quarantine. However, in discussing imports and exports, it recognizes the right of states to execute inspection laws, which are incident to the exercise of quarantine powers. In 1824, Chief Justice [John] Marshall suggested that states have authority to quarantine under their police powers. Since Marshall's time, courts have upheld the exercise of compulsory detention powers for public health purposes. This jurisprudence reveals deference by the courts, which usually regarded isolation or quarantine actions as presumptively valid. Judicial activity in U.S.

This poster was published around 1925 by the Rensselaer County Tuberculosis Association in Troy, New York, as part of their campaign to educate the public about TB transmission. Courtesy of the National Library of Medicine.

public health has primarily been driven by challenges mounted against the exercise of quarantine powers during epidemics, notably TB.

In these cases, the judiciary asserted some control over isolation and quarantine measures. Following the "rule of reasonableness" established in *Jacobson v. Massachusetts*, courts insisted that use of quarantine powers be justified by "public necessity," and that states may not act "arbitrarily" or "unreasonably." Courts have also set four limits on isolation and quarantine authority:

1. The Subject Must Be Actually Infectious or Have Been Exposed to Infectious Disease. Health authority must demonstrate that individuals are infected or were exposed to disease and, thus, pose a public health risk. Courts have been reluctant to stigmatize citizens in the absence of reasonable proof. Thus, isolation of persons with TB must demonstrate that they are infectious, or would be infectious if they stopped taking their medication.

2. Safe and Habitable Conditions. Courts periodically insisted on safe and healthful environments for those subject to isolation or quarantine because public health powers are designed to promote well-being, and not to punish. The Supreme Court held, for example, that civilly committed mental patients have a right to "conditions of reasonable care and safety," "freedom from bodily restraint," and "adequate food, shelter, clothing and medical care.". . .

3. Justice and Non-Discrimination. A federal court struck down one of the most invidious measures in public health history in *Jew Ho v. Williamson*. At the turn of the 20th century, public health officials quarantined an entire district of San Francisco, ostensibly to contain an epidemic of bubonic plague, but the quarantine operated exclusively against the Chinese community. The federal court held the quarantine unconstitutional because health authorities acted with an "evil eye and an unequal hand." *Jew Ho* forms part of the leitmotif [theme] noted earlier—that governments are sometimes tempted to use their quarantine powers as an instrument of prejudice against vulnerable individuals or populations. This theme informed controversies that arose during MDR-TB [multidrug-resistant tuberculosis] outbreaks in the 1990s when New York and other cities targeted the mentally ill, drug addicts, and homeless persons for DOT, while affluent groups were spared. . . .

4. Procedural Due Process. Persons subject to detention are entitled to procedural due process. As the Supreme Court recognized, "[T]here can be no doubt that involuntary commitment to a mental hospital, like involuntary confinement of an individual for any reason, is a deprivation of liberty which the State cannot accomplish without due process of law." The procedures required depend on the nature and duration of the restraint. Certainly, the government must provide elaborate due process for long-term, non-emergency detention. Noting that "civil commitment for any purpose constitutes a significant deprivation of liberty," and that commitment "can engender adverse social consequences," the Supreme Court has held that, in a civil commitment hearing, the government has the burden of proof by "clear and convincing evidence."

In *Greene v. Edwards*, the West Virginia Supreme Court held that persons with infectious TB are entitled to similar procedural protections as persons with mental illness facing civil commitment. These safeguards include the right to counsel, a hearing, and an appeal. The invasion of liberty occasioned by detention, the implications of erroneously finding a person dangerous to the public's health, and the value of procedures in determining complex facts justify rigorous procedural protections.

The limits courts have placed on government use of isolation and quarantine reflect not only the threat posed by pathogenic microbes but also the rule of law. Whether and how isolation and quarantine are applied reveals aspects of politics, economics, and cultures in many societies. The relationship of quarantine powers to the rule of law is similarly instructive about governance strategies to balance individual rights and the public good. Jurisprudence on isolation and quarantine reveals a way of thinking about how political power should be, at each step, subject to legal rules and procedures. . . .

The Ethics of Involuntary Detention

Civil libertarians draw attention to the substantial personal interests affected by isolation and quarantine actions. Individuals subjected to confinement lose their liberty, suffer invasions of individual rights (including loss of privacy), face stigma because their community is aware of the infectious danger they pose, may have their bodily integrity compromised because of compulsory treatment, and endure socio-economic burdens such as the loss of income during their detention, and possibly thereafter. These issues are important individual interests, and state and federal governments should do all they can to mitigate these harms, as well as ensure that they exercise quarantine powers in accordance with the rule of law.

From an ethical perspective, the fact that detention is a drastic measure does not mean that isolation and quarantine are inappropriate. Persons with infectious, or potentially infectious, TB pose a risk to the public. TB can be spread by airborne droplets among persons congregated in confined spaces for extended durations, including long-haul travel in a bus, metro, train, or plane, as well as in group settings such as mental institutions, hospitals, nursing homes, and homeless shelters. Consequently, detention may be ethically justifiable, and provided that it is necessary, it is used as a last resort and applied in keeping with notions of human dignity and natural justice.

[Andrew] Speaker's case is an example of an ethically appropriate exercise of isolation powers. He had infectious TB. Whether his infectious TB was XDR-TB [extremely drug-resistant tuberculosis], as previously thought, or MDR-TB, as eventually diagnosed, does not change the ethical (or the epidemiological) analysis. Public health authorities first attempted less restrictive measures, such as treatment combined with "no travel" instructions, but twice Speaker did not comply and put the health of others at risk. Further, the federal government offered Speaker the opportunity to exercise his right to a hearing, a right guaranteed by the Constitution if not the existing FQR [federal quarantine regulations]. In each location of isolation, Speaker has been detained in highly therapeutic, humane facilities. Disagreements about the "facts" of his case do not change these conditions of ethical confinement: a dangerous infectious condition, less drastic alternatives attempted, procedural due process offered, and humane conditions of isolation.

In the ethical realm, Speaker's behavior raises another facet of the dynamics of isolation and quarantine in modern societies—the responsibility of individuals in the increasingly challenging and dangerous world of public health governance. Isolations of infectious TB patients typically, if not universally, involve failure of the patients to heed instructions concerning treatment or interacting with other persons. Government officials do not today blow the ram's horn to warn of contagious disease in the community, but warnings about appropriate individual behavior are given in ways that trigger ethical, if not legal, responsibilities of citizens to do no harm to others.

| "Partnerships, coalitions, and alliances, international, national, and local, are an ascendant form of organized response in public health."

International Cooperation Is Needed to Combat Resurgent Diseases

Jack C. Chow

Jack C. Chow is a medical doctor who has served as a senior advisor for global health policy and a U.S. ambassador for global HIV/AIDS. The following viewpoint is from a speech he made to the Canadian parliament when he was the assistant director-general of the World Health Organization for HIV/AIDS, Tuberculosis, and Malaria. In it he argues that cooperation and partnerships among governments at all levels is needed to effectively fight global diseases.

As you read, consider the following questions:

1. What contributions has the Canadian government made to the global fight against AIDS, tuberculosis, and malaria, as cited by Chow?

Jack C. Chow, "Remarks before the Parliament of Canada, Subcommittee on Human Rights and International Development," Canadian Parliament, Number 002, 3rd Session, 37th Parliament, April 28, 2004. www.stoptbnow.org. Reproduced by permission.

2. How can improved technical support assist in combating diseases worldwide, in the author's opinion?

3. According to Chow, how can the public health sector help people achieve the right to enjoy the "highest attainable standard of health"?

We [the World Health Organization (WHO)] welcome the effort by the Government of Canada to pass legislation that would enable safe, effective, low-cost generic medicines to be exported to areas of need. We value the contributions by the research-based pharmaceutical companies to add to the ARV armamentarium [antiretroviral tools and strategies].

Moving forward, we aim to knit an even closer relationship with Canada to identify new pathways of innovation. This is needed now more than ever as the three pandemics [AIDS, tuberculosis, and malaria] continue to spread.

More Public Effort Needed

Collectively, these three diseases kill 6 million people annually, a toll that is growing, especially in resource-poor countries: Three million from HIV-AIDS, two million from tuberculosis [TB], and one million from malaria.

For each of them, there are proven, effective interventions for prevention and treatment that can and must be scaled up. In addition to the expertise on medicine and public health provided by WHO, we also recognize the need for a strong, robust contribution by civil society and the need for political commitment at national and community levels.

A critical linkage was made between international development and public health, less than three years ago [circa 2001], by the declaration of a series of eight "Millennium Development Goals" articulated by heads of state at the United Nations.

The Millennium Development Goals (MDGs) provide important milestones towards the progressive attainment of access to basic health care. They cover areas that directly concern the work of WHO: reducing child mortality; improving maternal health; combating HIV/AIDS, TB, malaria, and other diseases; and improving access to water and sanitation, as well as access to essential drugs at affordable prices.

A Chain of Public Support

With the MDGs the international community set ambitious targets. To spur action to attain them, we believe what is needed is a strong chain of *concerted action* of all actors in the public health arena.

This chain can be thought of has having three basic links:

Link 1: Commitment from financial institutions and donors. After years of unwavering activism, more financial resources are being allocated to fight HIV/AIDS, TB and malaria. WHO applauds the advances made by our partners: Global Fund (US$5 billion), PEPFAR (US$15 billion), Gates Foundation (US$27 billion in assets), and the World Bank (US$2 billion). The growing roster of bilateral donors, including Canada, is contributing much needed resources. Canada has actively supported the creation of the Global Fund and so far has pledged US$100 million to it.

Link 2: Need for high quality technical support. As more resources are made available to fight the diseases, the challenge of providing quality and sustaining technical support is more important than ever. This includes working with governments, but also coordinating the different actors working on the ground.

WHO delivers this much needed assistance to countries in an effort to maximize use of valuable resources. We provide technical leadership and excellence through a combination of norms and standard setting, consensus building, a neutral and trusted voice, and recruiting and fielding of international staff. Therefore, WHO is uniquely positioned to ensure that money to fight diseases is well spent on effective strategies.

Public vs. Private Sector Disease Treatment in India

The average cost per patient successfully treated in the Public-Private Mix Directly Observed Treatment Systems project is US$ 144. The large reduction in costs incurred by patients and attendants when patients shift from the private non-DOTS sector to PPM-DOTS means that, from a societal perspective, PPM-DOTS results in both a reduction in total costs and an increase in effectiveness.

Costs/Effects/Cost-Effectiveness	PPM-DOTS project	Private non-DOTS sector
Total cost	44,161	61,475
Total number of cases successfully treated	306	179
Average cost per patient sucessfully treated	144	343

TAKEN FROM: Katherine Floyd, "Cost and Cost-Effectiveness of Public-Private Mix DOTS," World Health Organization, 2004.

WHO has the mandate and responsibility from the international community to support countries in their efforts to face public health challenges. Such legitimacy and trust underpins our capacity to convene donors and recipients alike to plan and coordinate an effective response.

Also within this link are key providers of technical support at the global and country level such as CIDA [Canadian International Development Agency] and Health Canada. We work closely with them and believe that they, too, ought to be as fully resourced.

Link 3: Strong collaboration with implementing partners. The collective response must be comprehensive and sustainable, not just to the individual challenge posed by a single disease, but also to build a lasting public health infrastructure that is sufficiently robust to confront a number of challenges.

Partnerships, coalitions, and alliances, international, national, and local, are an ascendant form of organized response in public health. Equally important is assuring that health systems are built with sufficient resources to confront future health crises effectively. . . .Canada has shown the way in creating innovative means to attain these goals, through its ground-breaking support of the Global Drug Facility [GDF]. The results are so impressive that the GDF is now serving as a model for the development of similar initiatives for HIV/AIDS and malaria medications.

The investment in building this strong, coherent chain helps convert resources into results. . . .

Global Programs

As the subcommittee has human rights in its mandate, let me spend a few minutes addressing this profoundly important area.

Human rights have been a core value of WHO's work since its inception.

In 1946, the creators of WHO's Constitution stated that the enjoyment of the highest attainable standard of health is a fundamental right of every human being. Our commitment to *Health for All* sets out the right to health as a guiding principle of WHO.

The health sector has an important obligation and contribution to ensure that testing, counselling, prevention, and treatment are accessible to those who need them most urgently, and that global efforts to increase access to these interventions also seek to dispel stigma and discrimination. Greater accountability to and stronger relationships with civil society groups and people living with the diseases are important elements in reaching these objectives.

We also found that effective interventions are failing to reach the most vulnerable groups. At the heart of the primary health care and the *Health for All* movement, which has been so influential in shaping health policies globally, lies a concern for equity. But, we all know that in every country groups of people miss out on what our health systems have to offer. The human rights framework can help us address the needs of these groups.

The task ahead is enormous and will grow even larger. We at WHO are committed to advancing the campaigns against AIDS, TB, and Malaria to the fullest extent possible.

"Much less attention had been given to the search for a malaria vaccine before the Gates Foundation invested more than $150 million in the effort."

Private Philanthropies Can Help Combat Resurgent Diseases

Tom Paulson

Tom Paulson has been the science and medical reporter for the Seattle Post-Intelligencer since 1987. He spent a month in Africa investigating the programs funded by the philanthropic foundation of Bill and Melinda Gates. He asserts that in 2000, the foundation spent 750 million dollars to launch the Global Alliance for Vaccines and Immunizations and that each year the foundation donates more than 1.5 billion dollars to global and national health and education programs. Such philanthropies go a long way toward combating global diseases, as Paulson reports.

As you read, consider the following questions:

1. What is the main goal of the Grand Challenges in Global Health Project, as cited by Paulson?

Tom Paulson, "$450 Million in Gates Grants Aims to Help Poor Nations Fight Disease," *Seattle Post-Intelligencer*, June 28, 2005. http://seattlepi.nwsource.com. Reproduced by permission.

2. According to the author, what is one way scientists hope to remedy the lack of childhood vaccinations in poor countries?

3. What is one point of criticism of the Gates Foundation that Paulson mentions?

British researchers plan to alter the genes of disease-causing mosquitoes, a Nobel laureate in California wants to use stem cell injections to replace vaccines and a Seattle bioengineer hopes to see his hand-held diagnostic device soon at work in remote Africa.

It's all because of a $450 million initiative started by Bill Gates, and co-managed by the Foundation for the National Institutes of Health [NIH], called Grand Challenges in Global Health.

The Bill & Melinda Gates Foundation and the NIH announced the recipients of $437 million in competitive grants that were awarded to 43 scientific teams in 33 countries. The project is aimed at enlisting the best and brightest in science to address some of the most critical technical obstacles to improving health throughout much of the developing world.

Nearly $50 million will go to Seattle organizations already playing leading roles in global health.

Money for Prevention and Diagnosis

Two malaria researchers at Seattle Biomedical Research Institute, Dr. Patrick Duffy and Stefan Kappe, received $19 million and $13.5 million, respectively, to continue their efforts aimed at finding an effective vaccine against the parasite that causes the disease.

"This will allow us to put together a much more comprehensive program," said Duffy, who spoke from Tanzania where he and his colleagues are studying malaria in pregnant women. Duffy came to Seattle Biomedical in 2001 because of a $5 million Gates grant that helped create what is now one of the largest malaria research programs in the nation.

Paul Yager, a University of Washington professor of bioengineering, received $15.4 million. Yager plans to develop a blood-testing device that will immediately diagnose diseases in poor communities lacking basic laboratory and medical equipment.

"You can manufacture these things for pennies," said Yager, holding up a prototype of the credit-card-sized blood analyzer he will develop in collaboration with other Seattle partners— PATH, an international health organization, Micronics, a medical device company in Redmond [Washington], and Nanogen, a Bothell [Washington]-based subsidiary of a San Diego diagnostics firm.

Vaccinating Children Everywhere

The Grand Challenges initiative, first announced by Gates at the World Economic Forum in 2003, was created because much of science neglects Third World problems.

"Unfortunately, the scientific efforts at creating modern medicine have largely ignored the diseases (of poor countries)," said Dr. Richard Klausner, director of the global health program at the Seattle philanthropy.

"There are 27 million children in the world who fail to receive appropriate immunizations every year and that's largely because of deficiencies in the current immunization programs," said Dr. Harold Varmus, president of Memorial Sloan-Kettering Cancer Center and head of the initiative's scientific advisory board.

Asking scientists to fix these deficiencies—by combining many vaccines into a single dose that can be given soon after birth, by developing vaccines that don't require refrigeration or finding alternatives to needle delivery—was a top priority.

A New Focus on Malaria

Discovering new vaccines against scourges such as HIV, malaria and tuberculosis was another. Although there has been a considerable amount of work done in the search for an AIDS

Malaria Fact Sheet

- In Africa, a child dies from malaria every thirty seconds.

- Malaria fatalities increased in the last two decades of the 20th century.

- There are at least 300 million acute cases of malaria each year, which result in more than a million deaths.

- Approximately 90% of deaths attributed to malaria occur in Africa.

- Malaria is Africa's leading cause of under-five mortality and it constitutes 10% of the continent's overall disease burden.

- The report estimates that investments in malaria R&D [research and development] totaled $323 million in 2004 or 0.3% of total health-related R&D investments. Yet malaria's impact on humanity is roughly 10 times that amount, accounting for 3.1% of global disease burden.

- The US National Institute of Allergy and Infectious Diseases (NIAID) and the Bill & Melinda Gates Foundation provided 49% of total malaria R&D investments in 2004. NIAID provided roughly $80 million, while the Foundation provided close to $78 million.

Malaria R&D Alliance, 2005.
www.malariaalliance.org.

vaccine, much less attention had been given to the search for a malaria vaccine before the Gates Foundation invested more than $150 million in the effort.

"Yet malaria kills at least a million people every year," noted Kappe.

Although Duffy and his colleagues are looking for vaccine targets by analyzing natural immunity among Tanzanian women and children, Kappe is genetically altering the parasites to see if a mutant form of the bug might be useful as a vaccine.

"We find that when we disrupt some genes, the parasite becomes attenuated (slightly disabled) and cannot cause infection," he said. But in experiments on mice, it does appear to stimulate immunity to further infections, Kappe said.

The Gates grant, he said, will allow Seattle Biomedical researchers to expand their search of the 5,000 or so genes in the malaria parasite to find the best ones to disrupt for a mouse malaria vaccine.

"Once we identify this in the rodent model, we will go to humans," Kappe said.

The Best Use of Funds?

Other top priorities for the Grand Challenges initiative include improving the nutritional values of staple foods such as rice, cassava, bananas and sorghum, short-circuiting the disease-spreading nature of mosquitoes and improving drug therapies for chronic infections. One grant recipient, Nobel Prize winner David Baltimore at the California Institute of Technology, received $13.9 million to explore using genetically engineering stem cells to boost immunity in people with HIV. If Baltimore's approach works for HIV, perhaps a patient's stem cells could be "pre-programmed" to protect against any infectious disease.

"It's an extremely interesting idea. . .that literally proposes to replace vaccines entirely," Klausner said.

But Baltimore's project also sounds especially speculative and unlikely to produce anything that will, in the near term, help the millions of people dying now from mundane diseases such as diarrhea or fever.

A number of public health experts have expressed concern that the Gates Foundation is becoming too enamored of "upstream" scientific projects and is moving away from its original emphasis of expanding the use of health tools already available—such as basic vaccines or drug therapies—to prevent disease and save lives now.

Klausner rejected such criticism, noting that the $450 million for Grand Challenges amounts to only about 8 percent of the philanthropy's total projected global health budget [through 2010].

"We don't see this as a sign of our walking away from the commitment to solving problems of global health as quickly as possible," said Klausner, noting that the foundation has given $1.5 billion to the Global Alliance for Vaccines and Immunization to greatly expand the number of children getting basic immunizations.

"We have a broad range of activities that run from delivering health tools now. . .to investing to create health tools that are needed but we don't have now," he said.

Periodical Bibliography

The following articles have been selected to supplement the diverse views presented in this chapter.

Lori Arnold — "Mandatory HPV Vaccine Bill Advances to California State Senate," *Christian Examiner Online*, July 2007. www.christianexaminer.com.

Biswajeet Banerjee — "Muslim Clerics Fighting Polio in India," Associated Press, November 12, 2006. www.ap.org.

Economist — "More Money than Sense," July 7, 2007.

Richard Harris — "Pandemic Flu Spurs Race for New Vaccine Methods," *NPR Morning Edition*, December 6, 2005. www.npr.org.

Paul Hunt — "Poverty, Malaria, and the Right to Health: Exploring the Connections," *UN Chronicle*, December 2007. www.un.org.

Hyung-Jin Kim — "All Poultry in Seoul Killed After Bird Flu Outbreak," Associated Press, May 12, 2008. www.ap.org.

Andrew Pollock and Stephanie Saul — "Merck to Halt Lobbying for Vaccine for Girls," *New York Times*, February 21, 2007.

David Rogers — "Docs: 'We Are Due' for Flu Outbreak," *Palm Beach (FL) Daily News*, April 12, 2008.

Sabin Russell — "Flu Pandemic Warnings Rated Like Hurricane Alerts," *San Francisco Chronicle*, February 2, 2007.

Harris Whitbeck and Fabiana Frayssinet — "Brazilian Military Joins Battle Against Dengue Epidemic," CNN, April 5, 2008. www.cnn.com.

How Can Resurgent Diseases Be Controlled?

Chapter Preface

Killer nanorobots are the ultimate dream of villainous scientists and their cohorts. They are the stuff that science fiction is made of! Right now, however, a *benevolent* team of computer and robot engineers and biomedical researchers from Australia, the United States, and Brazil are developing models for hardware and software systems that would allow future nanorobot technology to alert epidemiologists, doctors, and other public health personnel to the presence of minute quantities of infectious pathogens in a disease carrier so that they can prevent an illness from becoming a pandemic. With such technology, nanorobots could also track viruses and bacteria inside the body and dispense medication directly into the bloodstream.

Nanotechnology such as this is years away from practical (or even experimental) application, but developing outlines for its implementation is a useful exercise. The task of identifying ways to use nanotechnology in health care may even attract the help of scientists, researchers, engineers, and others previously uninterested in health care. To paraphrase Louis Pasteur, the nineteenth-century microbiologist who developed a vaccine for rabies, chance favors the prepared community; diseases often unexpectedly appear in populations, and a town or city that does not have a combat strategy in place loses valuable time developing one when it could have been treating the disease instead. Running simulations to prepare emergency workers for public health outbreaks is already commonplace; health care personnel participate in real-life simulations with road blocks, staging areas, and actors playing the role of victims. Although computer simulations are not so hands-on, they can model outbreaks at the cellular level in different scenarios and provide multiple opportunities to test different strategies with minimal effort and expense.

Since government policy and community leaders can manage public health only to a certain extent, some believe that people need to know how to take care of themselves instead of waiting for doctors and epidemiologists to find them when illness strikes. Public awareness campaigns about general health and specific diseases provide information to individuals about how to avoid contagion, what items (such as face masks) can slow or stop the spread of a bacterium or virus, what symptoms one can look for, and where one can go for help and protection in case of an outbreak or epidemic. It is possible that the people who pay attention and follow recommended guidelines for disease management are the people who stay healthier or receive treatment faster as the disease progresses through a community.

Private organizations play a role in disease management and containment, too. Nonprofit groups, including churches and charities, often raise funds to buy and distribute tools that protect individuals or finance the cost of screening for and treating diseases. Media corporations provide free broadcast time and billboard space to health groups so they can reach wider audiences. Health care professionals volunteer their time to share information at schools or job sites. Some employers even accommodate work schedules to allow sick employees to stay home and make up lost time later so they do not lose wages but do not make everyone else sick.

The following chapter explores some solutions that individuals, the government, and private organizations have devised to lessen the frequency of disease outbreaks and minimize the effects when they do occur.

> *"The WHO, USAID, Archbishop Tutu and hundreds of doctors and disease experts support the use of DDT for malaria control."*

DDT Is the Best Way to Control Malaria

Paul K. Driessen

Paul K. Driessen is a senior fellow with both the Committee for a Constructive Tomorrow and the Center for the Defense of Free Enterprise, nonprofit public policy institutes that focus on energy, the environment, economic development, and international affairs. He is also the author of Eco-Imperialism: Green Power, Black Death, *a book about the conflicts between the environmental movement and global humanitarian and energy programs. In the following viewpoint Driessen argues that the insecticide dichloro-diphenyl-trichloroethane, known commonly as DDT, is the most effective way to kill and control the mosquitoes that transmit malaria to human populations, thus controlling the spread of the disease.*

Paul K. Driessen, "The Truth About Malaria and DDT," *Eco-Imperialism*, July 17, 2006. www.eco-imperialism.com. Reproduced by permission.

As you read, consider the following questions:

1. What were the results of the recent implementation of DDT programs in South Africa, Swaziland, Mozambique, and Zambia, as reported by Driessen?

2. Why did the Environmental Protection Agency administrator ban DDT, according to the author?

3. What does Driessen say was one flaw of the study about the effects of DDT on the eggshells of wild birds?

Malaria continues to be the biggest single killer of African children. However, years of effort to improve malaria control programs are finally bearing fruit.

Archbishop Desmond Tutu, Greenpeace co-founder Patrick Moore, and hundreds of physicians, clergy and human rights advocates signed the Kill Malarial Mosquitoes NOW declaration, demanding that substantial funds be spent on indoor spraying with DDT, Artemisia-based combination therapies (ACT drugs), bed nets and other commodities—not just on conferences, reports, education and "capacity building," as important as those things also are.

In response to legislation enacted by the United States Congress, the U.S. Agency for International Development [USAID] is buying commodities and assisting with spraying programs. The new director of the World Health Organization's [WHO's] global malaria program has announced that indoor spraying with DDT will be an integral component of WHO's comprehensive new strategies. And mining and other companies are conducting successful anti-malaria programs that take the same approach.

DDT is not a silver bullet. Bed nets, larvacides, other insecticides, education, medicines and other weapons are also essential. However, it is a vital component of a truly integrated program to control this devastating disease. Simply put, no other chemical—at any price—can do what DDT does.

DDT and the Stockholm Convention

WHO [World Health Organization] proposed and supports the continued use of DDT for disease vector control, under the Stockholm Convention on Persistent Organic Pollutants (POPs). The reason for the Organization's position is summed up by the recommendations of a WHO Malaria Expert Committee meeting in 1998:

> It is anticipated that for some time to come there will continue to be a role for DDT in combating malaria, particularly in the poorest endemic countries. Restrictions on DDT for public health use contained in a future Persistent Organic Pollutants Convention should therefore be accompanied by technical and financial mechanisms to ensure that effective malaria control is maintained, to at least the same level, through vector control methods that depend less on pesticides generally, and on DDT in particular.

WHO urges that a premature shift to less effective or more costly alternatives to DDT, without adequate preparation of the capacity of Member States (human, technical, financial), will not only be unsustainable but also have a negative impact on disease burden in the endemic countries.

World Health Organization, 2005.

Advantages of DDT

It is the cheapest, longest lasting, most effective repellant and insecticide known to man. Just spraying a tiny amount on the eaves and walls of a home, just once or twice a year, keeps 90% of mosquitoes from even entering. (Even just hanging a couple strips of DDT-impregnated cloth near the door keeps half of them from coming in.) It also irritates any that do enter, so they don't bite, and kills those that land.

It's like a huge bed net over an entire household. Equally important, used this way, DDT is absolutely safe for people and the environment. In fact, it won't even get into the environment.

This is the system that South Africa, Swaziland, Mozambique and Zambia used to slash malaria rates by 75% in less than two years. They were then able to get scarce ACT drugs to people who still got sick, and cut malaria disease and death rates by almost 95% in just three years.

Just think what a similar program could do for other countries. Kenya alone loses 34,000 children below age 5 every year to malaria, according to Health Minister Charity Ngilu. (Uganda endures 70,000 deaths annually.) People who have to stay home from work because they have malaria, or must care for family members who have malaria, cost Kenya 170 million working days and billions of shillings each year.

Imagine reducing that by 75% or more in Kenya alone. Over 25,000 children would live to become future farmers, scientists, political leaders, teachers, musicians and businessmen. Parents could work an additional 127 million days a year. Kenya would be far more healthy and productive. And this amazing success story could be repeated in communities and countries all over Africa.

No wonder my colleagues and I have been absolutely stunned by some of the letters and articles that have appeared recently in Kenyan and Ugandan papers. They contained some of the most fallacious claims we have ever seen regarding DDT. They would be hilarious—if so many lives weren't at stake, and the claims weren't damaging Africa's recent progress in disease control. Here are the facts.

DDT Is Safe

Millions of soldiers and civilians were sprayed right on their bodies with DDT during and after World War II, to prevent malaria and typhus. After the war, DDT was sprayed in massive quantities all over the USA and Europe, to completely eradicate malaria in those countries. Millions of people (including me) played, swam or ate picnics in clouds of DDT.

World-renowned DDT expert Dr. Gordon Edwards used to eat a spoonful of DDT when he gave lectures about it. He finally died, at age 85—of a heart attack, while hiking in the mountains.

No deaths, cancers or other harm (except skin rashes) were ever demonstrated. Not one replicated scientific study ever found that DDT causes abortions, birth abnormalities, cancer or reduced fertility in humans. US Environmental Protection Agency Administrator William Ruckelshaus banned DDT, despite his own commission's conclusion that DDT was safe for people and the environment. He never attended even one hour of the commission's extensive hearings, never read even one page of its report, and later said his decision was "political," not scientific.

In fact, the worst thing anti-pesticide activists like Greenpeace even say today is: "*some* researchers *think* DDT *could* be inhibiting lactation and *may* contribute to lactation failure and low birth weights in babies." Compare those far-fetched and minor risks to the reality of countless mothers and babies dying from malaria.

[American author of *Silent Spring*] Rachel Carson did die from cancer, but there is no evidence that it was caused by DDT. Cancer is primarily a disease of middle-aged and old people in developed countries. Tragically few Africans will have to worry about it, because far too many will die long before they get cancer, from malaria and other diseases that DDT could help prevent.

As to birds, the only evidence that DDT causes thin egg-shells came from faulty experiments in which birds were fed only 20% of their required calcium. When Dr. Bittman did his studies again with proper calcium levels, the eggshells were normal. Ms. Carson worried about a silent spring—but there never was one anywhere in America. Even when she wrote her book, our bird populations were *increasing*. . . .

Today, DDT is manufactured in one facility in India and one in China. It has not been produced in the United States for nearly 35 years, and we don't export it anywhere.

As malaria and DDT expert Professor Donald Roberts of the Uniformed Services University of the Health Sciences, points out, no WHO report claims that DDT causes brain or other tumors. Remember—the WHO, USAID, Archbishop Tutu and hundreds of doctors and disease experts support the use of DDT for malaria control. They would not do so if the chemical were so toxic.

The Environment vs. People

Yes, DDT can harm fish. But modern indoor spraying programs use tiny amounts of DDT, confine it to household walls, prevent its use in agriculture, and keep it from reaching lakes and rivers.

Yes, the European Union and certain European companies and activists have threatened trade sanctions against African countries that use DDT. That is unconscionable—but an easy position for them to take, since they no longer have malaria, thanks in large part to DDT.

Instead of bowing to their blackmail, though, all African nations should challenge these threats, which put paranoia about barely detectable traces of this life-saving chemical above the lives of African parents and children. Such attitudes should not be tolerated. Access to DDT is protected by the Stockholm Convention [a 2004 international agreement banning certain pollutants] and WHO, whose guidelines will ensure that it is used properly, to save lives and safeguard wildlife and the environment.

Friends of the Earth may say its strange notions of "sustainable development" should come first, as one writer asserts. But if its policies control decisions in Africa, the only thing that will be sustained is hundreds of thousands of unnecessary deaths from malaria, year after year.

DDT can be a vital part of the answer to malaria. It can save millions of lives—if we let it. Sound science and real environmental ethics demand that we do so.

> *"The risk of malaria for children . . . who received [cotrimoxazole] and used insecticide-treated bed nets was decreased by 97%."*

Preventive Drugs and Bed Nets Are the Best Way to Control Malaria

Theo Smart and Virginia Differding

Theo Smart is a consultant editor for NAM, a United Kingdom-based organization that creates and disseminates information about AIDS. Virginia Differding works in the field of international public health as a medical writer for publications on the treatment of HIV and as a program manager for international health initiatives. In the following viewpoint Smart and Differding summarize research findings presented at the Fourteenth Conference on Retroviruses and Opportunistic Infections by Dr. Anne Gasasira, an AIDS researcher in Uganda. The findings reveal that using a preventive drug regimen and bed nets treated with insecticide provide extremely effective prevention against malaria-carrying mosquitoes.

As you read, consider the following questions:

1. What are some concerns of Dr. Gasasira, as cited by Smart and Differding, about relying on drugs to prevent malaria?

2. What methods do the authors report were used to track the effectiveness of drug treatments and bed net use against malaria?

3. According to Smart and Differding's report, why were bed nets eventually distributed to all children, regardless of what experiment group they were in?

Providing HIV-infected children in Uganda with insecticide-treated bed nets (ITNs) and cotrimoxazole prophylaxis (CTX) [a combination of preventive antibiotics] dramatically reduces their risk of acquiring malaria according to results from the CHAMP (Children with HIV and Malaria Project) in Kampala, [Uganda,] presented at the Fourteenth Conference on Retroviruses and Opportunistic Infections in Los Angeles [in 2007].

This prospective study looked at malaria incidence within a cohort [group] of HIV-positive children who received cotrimoxazole (CTX) and ITNs compared to a concurrent cohort of healthy children who don't receive these interventions. Only nine episodes of malaria were reported in the HIV-positive children with CTX administration and use of treated bed nets. This represented a 97% reduction in incidence as compared to what occurred in the cohort of HIV-negative children (who were not given CTX and did not have access to ITNs until more than midway through the study) where 440 episodes of malaria were reported.

Two Overlapping Epidemics

HIV and malaria overlap substantially in sub-Saharan Africa. HIV is associated with an increased malaria incidence and morbidity in adults and pregnant women (particularly in those with advanced disease). Much less, however, is known about HIV's effect on malaria in children, the population most at risk of infection, with severe illness. Over a million children die of malaria each year, 75% of them in Africa.

"This lack of information [about children] is a critical gap in our understanding of the overlap between HIV and malaria," said Dr. Anne Gasasira, who presented the findings of CHAMP.

Nevertheless, interventions have recently become available in Africa that could significantly impact the risk of malaria in children with HIV. For example, CTX has activity against the malaria parasite and the use of CTX prophylaxis has been associated with decreased risk of malaria in HIV-infected adults.

At the same time, CTX is closely related to other antifolate antimalarials, such as *Fansidar* [a patented drug], and the use of CTX against malaria could be complicated by drug resistance. There is a possibility that CTX may not work in areas where resistance to *Fansidar* is widespread or, conversely, that widespread CTX use could increase the spread of *Fansidar* resistance and limit its effectiveness where it is still used (currently, primarily as a prophylaxis against malaria and placental malaria by pregnant women).

ITNs have also been shown to markedly reduce the risk of acquiring malaria—but the combined use of ITNs with CTX has not previously been studied.

The Bed Net Study

At Mulago Hospital in Kampala, 861 children aged one to ten were enrolled into the CHAMP study between October 2005 and September 2006 (300 HIV-infected children and 561 HIV-negative children randomly selected from the local community).

At the start of the study, 88% of the children with HIV were already using ITNs (and, as per policy, most if not all should have already been taking CTX as well) while none of

More Effective than DDT

Myth: DDT [insecticide dichloro-diphenyl-trichloroethane] is the best tool to fight malaria. *Fact*: The World Health Organization tried to eradicate malaria worldwide with a massive DDT spray program in the 1950s and 60s. While the program helped to control malaria in many places, wiping out malaria with DDT was an unrealistic goal that could not be met. One of the many reasons for the failure of this ambitious effort was resistance to DDT among malaria-carrying mosquitoes. Resistance was identified in Africa as early as 1955, and by 1972 nineteen species of mosquito worldwide were resistant to DDT. Often DDT intended for public health use is diverted to illegal agricultural use, hastening the development of resistant mosquito populations. More effective and safer approaches to malaria control are now being used in many countries. For example, Mexico uses an integrated approach that combines: a) early detection of malaria cases and prompt medical treatment, b) community participation in notification of malaria cases and cleaning of streams and other sites where mosquitoes breed; and c) low-volume chemical control with pyrethroid pesticides. [Pyrethroid pesticides disintegrate quickly in sunlight and do not affect groundwater.]

Pesticide Action Network North America, 2007.

the children in the community cohort were on CTX and only 6% reported use of bed nets at the start of the study.

Both cohorts were on identical assessment schedules for malaria. Parasite prevalence was measured at enrollment and every three months. Thick blood smears were performed on each child who presented in clinic with a new episode of fever. Clinical malaria was defined as fever (without other cause) and evidence of malaria parasites by microscopy.

Perhaps unsurprisingly (because many of the HIV-negative children were already receiving the interventions under evaluation) there was already a difference in malaria incidence at baseline: 113 (20%) of the HIV-negative children had positive malaria blood smears at study enrolment versus none of the HIV-infected children. Parasitaemia is quite common in this setting and not always associated with clinical malaria (especially in older children), but any child who developed clinical cases (with fever) would have been treated at the hospital and cured. However, children in areas with a high burden of malaria can get infected repeatedly.

Over the course of follow-up, all the HIV-infected children were all taking CTX and those who were not using ITNs at enrollment were given them, and those who qualified for antiretroviral therapy (ART) received treatment according to WHO [World Health Organization] guidelines. However, no HIV-negative child received cotrimoxazole, though by May and June, 2006, all were given bed nets for ethical reasons.

By the end of follow-up, 519 HIV-negative children and 290 HIV-positive children remained in the study. The gender distribution was similar in both groups and the age of the children with HIV was slightly younger (5.6 vs 6.5 years old). In the HIV-positive children, the median CD4% [the percentage of a certain type of T cell] was 21% (interquartile range 15–28%) and 35 [children] (12%) were on ART.

Evaluating Effectiveness

CTX reduced the incidence of malaria by 35%, though this was not statistically significant, while the use of ITN alone significantly reduced the incidence by 45%. The risk of malaria for children in the HIV-infected cohort who received CTX and used insecticide-treated bed nets was decreased by 97%.

Only nine episodes of malaria were reported in this cohort. Five of these episodes occurred in a small subset of HIV-positive children who were not initially using bed nets (and these occurred over a short period of time), while only four cases occurred in those with bednets from the start.

In the HIV-negative community group without cotrimoxazole (or bed nets for much of the study), there were 440 episodes of malaria;. . . 356 episodes occurred among those without any intervention. 84 cases occurred in HIV-negative children using bed nets.

This study establishes the efficacy of CTX administration and the use of treated bed nets in preventing malaria in the pediatric population with HIV.

This is highly significant given that the study took place in a malaria-endemic area with high-level antifolate (*Fansidar*) resistance. . . . One final and useful clinical observation was that malaria accounted for only 4% of all fever episodes in the HIV-infected cohort. Usually, 30–40% of fevers in this area are attributable to malaria. (In fact, in the HIV-negative children in this study, 33% of the fevers were associated with malaria.) Fever in children in the area is usually treated empirically for malaria.

Researcher Conclusions

"Our studies' findings support the use of CTX prophylaxis and ITNs for all HIV-infected children living in malaria endemic areas and this is regardless of HIV disease stage," said Dr. Gasasira. "And given the rarity of malaria in the setting of these preventative measures, we recommend that malaria therapy should only be given after laboratory confirmation."

> *"Evidence ... suggests that immunising a fraction of a community reduces the transmission of cholera sufficiently for the unvaccinated members of the community to benefit."*

Vaccinating Only Part of a Population Could Control Cholera

Lorenz von Seidlein

Lorenz von Seidlein is a senior lecturer at the London School of Hygiene and Tropical Medicine and at Mahidol-Oxford Tropical Medicine Research Unit in Bangkok, Thailand. He is also a staff member of the International Vaccine Institute in South Korea. In the following viewpoint Seidlein argues that evidence shows that cholera could be eradicated in areas where as few as 50 percent of a community were vaccinated, though more studies are needed. Results from studies decades old should not be relied upon in making policy for cholera control, he contends.

Lorenz von Seidlein, "Vaccines for Cholera Control: Does Herd Immunity Play a Role?" *PLoS Medicine*, vol. 4, no. 11, November 2007, pp. 1719–1721. http://medicine .plosjournals.org.

As you read, consider the following questions:

1. What are a few of the factors that might explain why the number of reported cases of cholera in Asia has decreased in recent history, according to Seidlein?

2. What are some characteristics mentioned by the author of a useful malaria vaccination drug for poor and rural areas?

3. According to mathematical research models cited by Seidlein, at what percentage of group vaccination could herd immunity protect all members of a group from cholera?

Cholera is a diarrhoeal disease caused by [the bacterium] *Vibrio cholerae* O1 and O[BA1]139, transmitted through the faeco-oral route. The disease occurs in outbreaks but can establish itself permanently. The full impact of the disease is difficult to assess. The currently preferred measure of disease burden, disability-adjusted life years, fails to capture the enormous impact of a cholera outbreak, which spares no age group and paralyses the economy in severely affected areas.

Disease Burden

The seventh cholera pandemic began in Indonesia in 1961 and spread quickly to other Asian countries, which became the epicentre[BA2] of cholera outbreaks. With the economic emergence of Asia the number of cholera cases reported from that region has decreased. There are several possible reasons to explain this decline. First, massive investment has been made in providing a safe water supply and in sanitation. Second, reporting of cholera has become less reliable, because global trade—especially trade in seafood—and tourism are negatively affected by cholera outbreak reports.

In 1970 *Vibrio cholerae* O1 E1 Tor invaded sub-Saharan Africa, which had not experienced cholera for more than 100 years. In 2006, Africa reported 234,349 cases of cholera to the

World Health Organization (WHO), accounting for 99% of the officially notified global cholera. Between 1995 and 2005, 66% of cholera outbreak reports to ProMedmail (a global electronic reporting system for outbreaks of emerging infectious diseases and toxins, run by the International Society for Infectious Diseases) came from sub-Saharan Africa. There is growing evidence of the large and increasing burden of cholera in Africa.

Most recently the US-led invasion of Iraq has been accompanied by a re-emergence of cholera in that country. As of September 2007, nearly 7,000 cholera cases from the Sulaymaniyah and Kirkuk Governates have been reported to WHO.

Cholera Control and Vaccines

Cholera was eliminated from the industrialized world through safer water supplies, better sanitation, and improved food hygiene. These have been the accepted control mechanisms for the disease, but as the emergence of cholera in Iraq illustrates, the provision of safe water and sanitation breaks down during wars and complex humanitarian emergencies. In addition to these crisis situations, cholera also thrives in the ever-increasing slums of some megacities such as Kolkata (formerly Calcutta), India, which are not quickly accessible to improvements in infrastructure.

In 2002, WHO mentioned for the first time the potential use of oral cholera vaccines in endemic [locally restricted] and epidemic situations. Up to that point cholera vaccines were recommended for individual travellers to endemic countries but not for public health use in endemic countries. Far from embracing vaccinations for cholera control, WHO experts recommended gaining more experience through demonstration projects. Since then, mass oral cholera vaccinations have been conducted in Beira, Mozambique, in Darfour, Sudan, and in Aceh, Indonesia. These projects demonstrated the feasibility and effectiveness of vaccination under actual public health conditions. A WHO meeting at the end of 2005 suggested that "... the use of oral cholera vaccines in certain endemic situations should be recommended...."

The slow acceptance of vaccines for cholera control is probably related to the poor performance of earlier generations of cholera vaccines made from phenol-killed whole-cell preparations of *V. cholerae* O1 organisms and administered by injection as two doses, two weeks apart. The vaccine offered about 50% protection for a short duration, was associated with painful local inflammatory reactions, and is no longer recommended for use.

Available Vaccines

Currently two cholera vaccines are internationally licensed: (1) Dukoral, consisting of inactivated whole cells of *V. cholerae* O1 combined with the B-subunit (BS-WC) of the cholera toxin, and (2) the live attenuated vaccine CVD 103HgR (Orochol or Mutacol). Both vaccines have an excellent safety profile and afford high rates of protection over several years. The companies producing each vaccine have been acquired by the publicly listed Dutch company Crucell. Only Dukoral is currently produced, and for this reason was used in the above-mentioned vaccination campaigns in Mozambique, Sudan, and Indonesia. Dukoral costs travellers more than US$10 per dose, and two doses two weeks apart are recommended for immunisation. Most tourists can afford this vaccine, and well-supported foundations can purchase this vaccine for interventions in larger populations. Yet Dukoral is likely to remain too expensive for governments of cholera-endemic regions to vaccinate at-risk populations. The technology on which Dukoral is based has previously been transferred to manufacturers in Vietnam, and has been more recently transferred to an Indian vaccine producer with certification to produce internationally licensed vaccines. There is therefore a justified hope that this vaccine candidate will become available internationally at an affordable price.

What Is "Herd Immunity"?

The principle of herd immunity states that if you reach a critical percentage of community immunity, typically between 85–95 percent, the herd effect will protect the remaining 10–15 percent without immunity. This 10–15 percent includes children who are too young to receive a vaccine, those who are unable to receive certain vaccinations due to contraindications (i.e., cancer, HIV) and those who unknowingly have a vaccine failure. A vaccine failure occurs when a person who is given a vaccine does not have an appropriate immune response to it, and thus is still unknowingly susceptible to the disease.

For each virus, statisticians are able to calculate the minimum percentage of community immunity necessary to achieve herd immunity and prevent an outbreak. Though we only need about 85 percent of the community to have immunity to rubella, smallpox and diphtheria to prevent an outbreak, diseases such as whooping cough (pertussis) and measles require at least 94 percent immunity.

Dr. Steven F. Hirsch, "Protecting the 'Herd':
Why Vaccinations Still Matter," Washington Parent,
August 2007. www.washingtonparent.com

The ideal cholera vaccine is safe and affords extended if not lifelong protection after a single dose. It can be stored for extended periods at room temperature and is in the same price range as vaccines included in the WHO Expanded Program on Immunization. Promising candidates approaching this ideal are under development. Peru-15, for example, is a live, attenuated vaccine candidate that has been found to be safe and immunogenic in infants and children in Bangladesh. Because cold storage presents a challenge for the use of this vaccine in tropical cholera endemic regions, a thermostable vaccine is under development. A promising live, attenuated cholera vaccine candidate is being developed by the Cuban Finley Institute (Camaguey, Cuba); this candidate is currently under evaluation in sub-Saharan Africa and could become available at an affordable price.

Herd Protection

With the current availability of one vaccine, the development of better candidates, and the endorsement of WHO, wider use of vaccines for cholera control looks promising. From a policy maker's perspective, it would be useful to know the level of vaccine coverage to aim for to control cholera in a community, and second, whether this approach is cost-effective.

Recent evidence for herd protection conferred by oral cholera vaccinations suggests that immunising a fraction of a community reduces the transmission of cholera sufficiently for the unvaccinated members of the community to benefit from reduced risk of disease. However, while it has become clear that oral cholera vaccine programs will be more cost-effective than previous trial data had suggested, the level of coverage required to control cholera remains unknown.

In a study published in [the November 2007] issue of *PLoS Medicine* Ira Longini and colleagues have mathematically simulated varying vaccine coverage levels in the Matlab region of Bangladesh using a historic vaccine trial dataset. Their simulations suggest that in a population in which 50% received an oral cholera vaccine, 93% of the overall population would be protected; this level of protection, the authors think, would result in control of cholera transmission. To make their model more generalisable, they modified the assumptions in a sensitivity analysis. For populations that have less natural immunity than Matlab, 70% coverage would likely be necessary to provide sufficient protection to control cholera.

If the authors are correct, an achievable goal of 50% vaccine coverage could protect high-risk populations suffering recurrent cholera outbreaks. This suggestion is highly encouraging, because 50% vaccine coverage has been achieved in earlier mass vaccination campaigns. Current problems in eradication of poliovirus illustrate how difficult it is to reach the last 10% of the population to drive coverage above 90%. Reaching only half of the population is comparatively easy.

What Remains to Be Done?

The findings of Longini and colleagues are encouraging, but policies tend to rely on actual field-derived data, not on models. The authors had access to one dataset from a trial conducted more than 20 years ago in the Bay of Bengal, a place considered at the time by cholera experts as the "home of cholera," probably not representative for the global cholera situation in 2007. More data from a variety of settings is now needed.

Based on the models provided by Longini and colleagues, we would expect that mass vaccination campaigns with reasonable coverage in isolated areas with stable populations should eliminate cholera for several years. In contrast, vaccination campaigns in urban slums with highly mobile populations could have a lower impact. Nothing is known about the impact of a combination of improved water supplies and sanitation with vaccination campaigns, which could be additive or synergistic. The key to a better understanding is close documentation of interventions and outcomes, which will allow us to confirm or reject Longini and colleagues' models.

> *"India has the technical expertise to de-velop a cholera vaccine, has some of the best certified vaccine manufactur-ing units in the world, [and] has a large population that would immensely benefit from a cholera vaccine."*

India Need Only Apply Available Technologies to Control Cholera

G. Balakrish Nair

G. Balakrish Nair is a prominent Indian microbiologist. He is the director of the National Institute of Cholera and Enteric Dis-eases (NICED) in Kolkata (formerly Calcutta), India. In the fol-lowing viewpoint, Nair argues that cholera rates in India could be controlled if India would use its newly found economic power and technological prowess in its own behalf by investing in vac-cine licensing and public health programs for its people.

As you read, consider the following questions:

1. What is the difference between reported cases of and deaths from cholera and the projected number of actual cases, according to Nair?

G. Balakrish Nair, "How Much More Research Is Required to Prevent Cholera?" *Indian Journal of Medical Research*, vol. 125, no. 5, May 2007, pp. 612–614. Copyright © In-dian Council of Medical Research. Reproduced by permission.

2. How have cholera infection patterns changed in Delhi, India, over the past fifty-six years, in the author's opinion?

3. What link does the author make between national sanitation programs and cholera incidence in North America and Europe?

In some parts of the world, cholera has been relegated to history books. Yet in most others, particularly in the developing and poorer parts of the world, cholera continues to remain a formidable challenge. Global statistics indicate that there has been a sharp increase in the number of cholera cases reported to WHO [World Health Organization] during 2005 with a total of 131,943 cases including 2272 deaths notified from 52 countries. The African continent, particularly west Africa, was badly hit in 2005, accounting for 95 percent of the global total of officially notified cholera cases. This trend has continued in 2006 with the disease ravaging Angola affecting 14 of the 18 provinces with an overall case fatality rate of about 4 percent, although in some provinces it reached 30 percent. Apparently, the burden of cholera in Asia would seem to be much lower than Africa but many Asian countries do not report their cases because of fears of unjustified travel and trade-related sanctions. How much of cholera is "swept under the carpet" in this region is anyone's guess. The true burden of cholera is probably several million cases in Asia and Africa with fewer cases in Latin America and an annual mortality of at least 40,000 to 100,000. There is a clear trend that cholera is re-emerging in parallel with the ever-increasing proportion of vulnerable populations who live in unsanitary conditions. This trend is attested to by an article by [researchers N.C.] Sharma and colleagues in [the May 2007] issue [of the *Indian Journal of Medical Research*] because it succinctly brings to light the problem of cholera over a period of time in Delhi. This report has several important messages.

Changing Seasonality

The changing seasonality of cholera observed in Delhi in the study of Sharma and co-investigators is a striking observation. They report that in 2003 cholera occurred in Delhi between April and October while in 2004 and 2005 cholera occurred throughout the year. The pattern of 2004 and 2005 completely contrasts previous trends in Delhi where cholera was described as a highly seasonal disease. In the 1950s, Delhi was described as a region which remained free from cholera for considerable periods. So with the passage of time Delhi has transformed from a region of rare occurrence, to seasonal occurrence, to a region which now has cholera cases throughout the year. And all this in a span of 56 years.

Cholera is a climate-sensitive disease and the dynamics of the disease fluctuates with variation in global and regional climate. Increasing temperatures (prediction of 1.4 to 5.8°C in the next 100 years) would be expected to expand the range and increase the prevalence of [cholera bacterium] *V. cholerae* and cholera both geographically and temporally if public health measures are not implemented. It has already begun to show in Delhi and many other parts where there has been a continuous surveillance confirming what the ecologist Andy Dobson at Princeton states: "A warmer world will be a sicker world" (*Newsweek*, "A Hot Zone for Disease," July 8, 2002). For the past 25 years we have been tracking another *Vibrio*, the halophilic seafood-borne pathogen *V. parahaemolyticus*, that causes gastroenteritis. A new genotype of *V. parahaemolyticus* has registered an alarming rise in global prevalence in the past 10 years [1997–2007] and is causing what some like to call "another *Vibrio* on a pandemic binge."

Antibiotic Resistance

Antibiotic therapy is a useful adjunct to fluid replacement in the treatment of cholera by substantially reducing the duration and volume of diarrhoea and thereby lessening fluid re-

Prevalence of Sanitation Facilities in India, 2003

	Percentage	
Sanitation System	Urban	Rural
Private domestic connection to sewage system	28.7	2.5
Shared domestic connection to sewage system	5.6	0.1
Private flush to septic tank	16.7	6.1
Shared flush to septic tank	8.8	0.8
Private pour flush latrine	15.0	4.3
Shared pour flush latrine	6.7	1.2
Private convered dry latrine (with privacy)	1.6	3.3
Shared covered dry latrine (with privacy)	1.5	0.6
Uncoverd dry latrine (without privacy)	0.3	1.7
Bucket latrine (where fresh excreta are manually removed)	1.5	0.9
No facilities (open defecation)	13.6	78.4
Other	0.0	0.1
Total	**100.0**	**100.0**

TAKEN FROM: WHO/UNICEF, "Urban and Rural Sanitation—India," Joint Monitoring Programme for Water Supply and Sanitation, June 2006. www.wssinfo.org.

quirements and shortening the duration of hospitalization. The antibiotic resistance pattern of the Delhi strains of *V. cholerae* is concerned with 96.6 percent of the strains being resistant to furazolidone (Fz), sulphamethoxazole-trimethoprim (TMP-SMX) and nalidixic acid. TMP-SMX and tetracycline (Te) are the antibiotics of choice in the treatment of cholera while Fz is an alternative antibiotic recommended in places where *V. cholerae* O1 or O139 are resistant to Te or TMP-SMX. Fortunately, most isolates of *V. cholerae* O1 and O139 in Delhi are still sensitive to Te which has been the mainstay for the treatment of cholera for the past 40 years. In Bangladesh, *V. cholerae* O1 has developed antimicrobial resistance to TMP-SMX, Fz and Te, and resistance is emerging to ciprofloxacin and azithromycin, leaving few options for effective antimicrobial treatment for cholera. Given that cholera spreads in waves across continents, it will not be too long [before] such multidrug resistant strains will appear globally. . . .

The Future

We have such a wealth of information on the epidemiology, ecology, clinical aspects, treatment, pathophysiology, pathogenic mechanisms, toxin biology, vaccinology and genomics of *V. cholerae* but yet the disease cholera continues to be a public health nightmare in many countries, including India. Humans are an integral part of the ecology of *V. cholerae*. The human intestinal milieu selects the pathogenic clone from a melange of organisms that enter through contaminated water or food, amplifies the clone and in the process causes the disease. The disease, in turn, is an efficient mechanism to disseminate the pathogen. If the excreta of cholera patients are not sanitarily disposed, just a single patient can disperse billions of toxigenic *V. cholerae* organisms into the environment and perpetuate the cycle. This is where we need to stop the cycle, which the West has done so very effectively and in doing so has eradicated cholera. In fact, cholera had spurred what we now term as the "sanitary revolution" in North America and Europe. Even though there are sporadic imported cases of cholera occasionally entering these countries, the chances of its spreading are non-existent because further transmission does not occur. In India, we must learn to accept that the occurrence of cholera is the collapse of sanitation and availability of clean water in the settings where it occurs. In fact, cholera should be used as an indicator for the breakdown of sanitation and public hygiene. Essentially, the human cycle has to be completely interrupted if we need to get rid of cholera. And there are two ways to do this. One is to find a way to stop the entry of *V. cholerae* into humans or the other is [to] make humans impervious to the disease. The former can be done by sanitation and provision of safe drinking water and the latter by an efficient vaccine. Ideally, all interventions should proceed in tandem.

There are at least three oral cholera vaccines available in the International market catering mainly [to] travellers but none in India and other countries where the vaccine is most needed. This is the paradox of cholera. India has the technical expertise to develop a cholera vaccine, has some of the best certified vaccine manufacturing units in the world, has a large population that would immensely benefit from a cholera vaccine but yet we do not have a cholera vaccine nor are the currently available oral cholera vaccines licenced in our country. While we are in the frontiers of research in many aspects of cholera, we are at the abysmal ebb of translating all this knowledge into useful public health tools that would control and prevent cholera. We need to put our act together; otherwise with cholera in our backyard the Indian economic miracle that we talk about will remain a myth.

"The overwhelming majority of [interviewed immigrants] welcomed screening and felt reassured by the process."

Most Immigrants Find Screening an Acceptable Way of Controlling TB's Resurgence

Penny Brewin et al.

Penny Brewin is a registered nurse in the Department of Respiratory Medicine at Homerton University Hospital in London. Her coauthors are all medical professionals in the United Kingdom. *In the following viewpoint they contend that despite the controversy surrounding the screening of immigrants to the U.K. for tuberculosis, deemed discriminatory by some opponents, the immigrants interviewed by them showed that such screening was largely acceptable and even welcomed.*

As you read, consider the following questions:

1. What was the purpose of studying how immigrants feel about tuberculosis screening programs, according to the authors?

Penny Brewin et al., "Is Screening for Tuberculosis Acceptable to Immigrants? A Qualitative Study," *Journal of Public Health Medicine*, vol. 28, no. 3, September 2006, pp. 253–258. Copyright © 2006 by the author. Reproduced by permission of the publisher and the author.

2. What locations in the United Kingdom do the authors say are currently available to provide tuberculosis screening tests to immigrants?

3. What specific conclusions do the authors draw from their study?

One-third of the world's population is infected with *Mycobacterium tuberculosis*, and an estimated 2 million people die from tuberculosis each year, largely in the developing world. Migration, drug resistance and HIV infection have contributed to the re-emergence of tuberculosis as a major public health problem in Europe and North America. Numbers of international migrants have more than doubled in the last 35 years to 175 million; one in every 35 people is an international migrant.

Screening immigrants for tuberculosis is controversial, generating considerable media, political and public health interest. Compulsory screening is a common policy. Screening is widespread in Europe, North America and Australia and is a prominent recommendation in guidelines, but has been criticized as being ineffective, poor value, discriminatory, stigmatising, racist and divisive. In the UK, tuberculosis screening is currently voluntary and takes place in port health units, hospital new entrant clinics, social services centres and primary care. Uptake of screening in hospital new entrant clinics is poor, with only one in five invited attending.

The debate on the role of tuberculosis screening of immigrants is poorly informed by data. Limited randomized trial data are available on the effectiveness of screening immigrants, with only observational and theoretical modelling studies guiding policy. Acceptability to recipients is universally acknowledged as an ethical prerequisite for any screening programme, the more so for programmes which may be compulsory and which target potentially vulnerable groups. Screening of immigrants for tuberculosis has been carried out for at least 50 years; yet, the views of recipients about acceptability remain unknown.

We addressed this omission by carrying out a qualitative interview study. Our aims were (i) to determine the acceptability of tuberculosis screening in immigrants attending for screening in different settings and (ii) to explore recipients' understanding of the disease and its relation to uptake of screening.

We considered 'acceptability' in this context to mean that the concept of being screened and the process, including the setting and procedure, were considered beneficial and tolerable by recipients. The setting for our study was east London, an area with an incidence of tuberculosis of 100/100,000 population, the highest in the UK. . . .

Acceptability of Screening

The overwhelming majority of informants welcomed screening and felt reassured by the process. This was expressed as a sense of security or relief, particularly after a negative screening result. Others saw screening as a 'privilege' and 'a good idea'. Being screened was seen as a socially responsible activity, reducing the chances of tuberculosis becoming a problem for the host country. Some felt that the wider settled population should also have access to screening. Others, interviewed with their families, felt that screening should be particularly promoted for children.

Because uptake of screening was almost universal at the social services and primary health care centres, and those attending the hospital new entrants clinic had already accepted a postal invitation to attend for screening, we identified only four people who had declined screening during the study. Even these four were not averse to screening *per se*: two thought it unnecessary, because they had been vaccinated with bacillus calmette-guérin (BCG) [against tuberculosis] or screened with tuberculin in their own countries, and two preferred to be screened by their general practitioners. Of the latter, one had multiple health problems and thought tuberculin testing might adversely affect his health and the other felt 'singled out' at the social services and felt that the general population should also get the protection of screening, not just asylum seekers.

Only two informants commented that they were selected for screening, because they were immigrants (one accepted, commenting that everyone should be screened, the other declined); both understood the invitation to reflect the high incidence of tuberculosis in their country of origin. None raised the possibility of a diagnosis of tuberculosis compromising an asylum application.

Although informants were positive about the purpose of screening a few expressed anxieties about the *process* of screening itself. These comments reflected insufficient explanation by screening staff. For one woman, screening raised anxieties about the lack of public health information.

Screening Setting

Informants were positive about the setting in which they had been seen, but not all settings were acceptable to all participants, suggesting that limiting the service to a single setting would reduce uptake. Primary care was 'easy', 'local' and appropriate, because screening was seen as less serious than treating the disease itself, which would be a matter of concern for the hospital. Some saw the general practice (GP) surgery as 'safer and cleaner', and another commented that they felt safer at the GP 'because you are familiar with him and the way [the surgery] works'.

The hospital was a good place to screen, because it was 'better equipped, with everything' with 'very specialized' staff. One respondent was more confident about being screened in hospital, because it was safer—in GP 'anything could happen'

The Forgotten Pandemic

Some 200 years ago, tuberculosis [TB] was a western-European export to the rest of the world. In the mid-1980s it was realised that the disease was out of control across most of the poorest regions of the world. In 1993 the WHO [World Health Organization] declared TB to be a world emergency.

Despite increasing intervention, cases are set to increase globally for the foreseeable future. Every two hours, as many people die from TB as have ever died from SARS [severe acute respiratory syndrome].

One third of the world's population, two billion people, are infected with the tubercle bacillus. It is estimated that deaths from TB will increase from the present level of two million a year to five million by the year 2050.

In the UK, cases have been increasing since 1987 and now number over 7,000 a year as a result of rising rates in developing countries, particularly Africa and the Indian subcontinent, and increasing travel to and from these countries. Case rates in the white UK-born population are around three in 100,000 a year, while rates in those born in India are 65 times and in those born in Africa 120 times higher.

Peter D. O. Davies, GP, July 14, 2006.

and there is 'only the doctor and they don't really know nothing'. Another pointed out that 'they have to transfer you' so going direct to the specialist was better.

Social services were 'easy and quick', because benefits (such as food vouchers) and screening were under one roof, and unlike the GP and hospital, there were no queues [waiting lines]. One man saw the benefits people were receiving at the centre as a useful way of increasing uptake of screening for a condition he thought people knew little about. Two were clear that they would not attend other settings: 'if you have to go to the GP for screening, we don't go'. A woman said she had no time to attend the hospital because of childcare responsibilities.

Understanding Tuberculosis and Accepting Screening

Explanatory models of tuberculosis held by our informants generally reflected notions about germs and infection. Most understood tuberculosis to be a disease affecting the chest; several identified it as one of a number of 'killer' diseases. Although many were unsure, most considered tuberculosis an infection that could affect the lungs. Understanding of transmission varied enormously. Ways of contracting tuberculosis included smoking cigarettes and hemp, touching people, sharing plates, glasses or cigarettes, mothers putting moistened food from their own mouths into their children's mouths, coughing, sexual contact (when tuberculosis developed from gonorrhoea), generally neglecting your health and not washing fruits and vegetables. Risk was raised at two levels, in relation to populations and individuals. Some population groups, such as the homeless or those in prison, were perceived to be at particular risk. Immunization was frequently cited as a preventive measure. Some informants were unclear about the distinction between BCG immunization and tuberculin testing; this may have been a factor in the decisions of the small number of those who declined screening. Most viewed tuberculosis as being treatable with long courses of medicine or injections.

Although several had heard that there were many cases in east London—either from word of mouth or from local newspapers—many highlighted the lack of information and education available in the media when compared with their country of origin and stated that their knowledge of the disease was based on what they had learnt from personal experience before entering the UK.

Responses of the participants at the focus group confirmed our interpretation of screening procedures in the three settings as being acceptable. Some commented that recipients might interpret screening that involved venesection [blood drawing] as covert testing for HIV infection.

Primary Findings

We found acceptability of screening for tuberculosis to be high amongst this diverse sample of immigrants offered voluntary screening in three different settings in east London. Even the few respondents who declined screening thought it a rational policy. This reflected high levels of awareness or personal experience of tuberculosis, particularly in people who were from countries of high tuberculosis incidence. Screening was acceptable in each of the three settings: respondents identified the advantages of tuberculosis screening in the location where they were approached and also reasons for not being screened in other settings.

The widespread understanding among our respondents of tuberculosis as a serious but preventable and treatable condition contributed to attendance for screening. The view that screening was unfairly targeted at immigrants was rare, even though we sought this in interviews.

Our findings are novel. We could not identify any reports on acceptability of screening for tuberculosis.

Our findings make four contributions to the debate about tuberculosis screening.

First, our data provide some reassurance that screening in these settings is viewed positively by recipients. Caution should be exercised in generalizing qualitative data. However, we recruited a diverse sample of respondents from a range of settings, and it seems reasonable to expect that the views of our sample might reflect those of other immigrants to the UK. We did not sample people being screened at port of entry; acceptability may differ in this setting.

Second, our data reinforce the importance of ensuring screening is as acceptable as possible to recipients. Resolving anxieties about the process and safety of screening by improving communication and information may increase acceptability further in few attenders. Improving the acceptability of any screening programme is not only a moral aim, but it may improve uptake and hence the cost-effectiveness of the screening.

Third, although people were generally happy with the setting in which they were screened, all settings were not acceptable to all recipients, suggesting that screening should be offered in a range of settings to maximize uptake.

Fourth, our data underline the need for and potential of more information for the general public about tuberculosis. Ideas about transmission of tuberculosis were highly varied, often superficial, and sometimes erroneous. It was striking that most informants had learned what they knew of tuberculosis from personal experience or public health campaigns in their countries of origin rather than in the UK.

> "The introduction of compulsory [screening] measures may mean that some patients may delay seeking care and pose a greater public health threat."

Compulsory Screening of Immigrants May Hinder Tuberculosis Control

Richard Coker

Richard Coker is head of the Communicable Diseases Policy Research Group, which focuses on the public health problems associated with international communicable disease control. He is also a lecturer at the London School of Hygiene and Tropical Medicine at the University of London in the United Kingdom. In the following viewpoint Coker analyzes the political argument to enact compulsory screening of all immigrants for tuberculosis and identifies potential problems and impracticalities, contending that such a program has too many negatives to be justified.

As you read, consider the following questions:

1. What is the purpose of screening immigrants for communicable diseases like tuberculosis, in Coker's opinion?

Richard Coker, "Compulsory Screening of Immigrants for Tuberculosis and HIV," *BMJ*, vol. 38, no. 7435, February 7, 2004, pp. 298–300. Copyright © 2004 British Medical Association. Reproduced by permission.

2. What, according to the author, is one logistical problem, from an administrative standpoint, with the tuberculosis screening test?

3. How do HIV and tuberculosis infections differ from a public health standpoint, according to Coker?

Increased movements of peoples are stressing public health responses to threats from communicable diseases internationally. [In 2004] several bodies in the United Kingdom, including the Conservative [political] party, have called for compulsory screening of immigrant populations for tuberculosis and HIV in order to support national efforts to control these communicable diseases. Given that concerns about asylum policy are consistently high on the political agenda, and that the media have recently taken to conflating anti-immigrant sentiments with public health threats through communicable diseases, the government may be considering compulsory screening of immigrants for some infectious diseases. But is there a rational public health argument that is grounded in evidence for compulsory screening of immigrants?

Poor Rationale for Screening

For tuberculosis and HIV the purpose of screening should be twofold—to identify cases early such that individuals can be offered treatment and care, and so to inhibit further transmission (through treatment, behaviour change, or isolation) to protect public health.

For tuberculosis the notion that screening immigrants detects those with the disease and therefore benefits public health is not straightforward. Although the increase in rates of tuberculosis in England and Wales over the past decade is clearly associated with immigrants, this does not translate into a cogent argument in favour of screening immigrants, never mind compulsory screening.

Most active tubercular disease seems to develop after immigration. Clearly, those individuals in whom tuberculosis is

Tuberculin Skin Test Problems

Reasons you may not be able to have the test or why the results may not be helpful include:

- A BCG (bacillus Calmett-Guérin) vaccination [against TB]. If you have had a BCG vaccination, you may have a positive . . . skin test.

- Taking medications that suppress the immune system, such as corticosteroids.

- Conditions that weaken the immune system, such as an HIV infection or cancer. The result also may be affected if a person is severely malnourished.

- Some vaccinations for infections, such as measles, mumps, rubella, polio, or chickenpox, given within 6 weeks before the tuberculin test. A recent infection with one of these viruses can also interfere with test results for a short period of time. The skin test also may be positive if the person has an infection caused by a mycobacterium other than the one that causes TB.

- A very recent TB infection. It takes 2 to 10 weeks for the immune system to react to TB bacteria.

- Age younger than 3 months old. A baby's immune system is not fully developed at this age.

- A "booster effect." This tends to occur in people who get regular TB skin tests, such as health care workers. The booster effect is a weak or no reaction to one TB skin test followed by a strong reaction from a second test. However, the strong reaction to the second test does not mean that the person has just become infected with TB.

Web MD, 2007. www.webmd.com.

identified early can benefit from treatment, but little evidence exists to show that early detection of tuberculosis in foreign born individuals conveys appreciable public health benefit to those born in the host country. This is not to say that people who live in close proximity might not be at greater risk, but that if the health of immigrant populations and those among whom recently arrived immigrants reside is the cause for concern then perhaps this should be an explicit rationale.

Current Programmes

Although current programmes of screening for active disease focus on asylum seekers, in whom prevalence rates are relatively high, very few active cases and fewer infectious cases are actually identified. Moreover, little correlation exists between the prevalence of disease in countries of origin and prevalence of active disease in those screened.

Given that immigrant groups other than those seeking asylum (including those who are undocumented, who are students, and who are seeking employment) have not traditionally been the focus of attention, a screening programme that attempts to encompass such diverse groups is likely to face substantial practical issues whether such a system is pre-entry, post-entry, or a combination of the two. Moreover, such a programme if implemented would be based on evidence with shallow foundations. An important practical problem in screening for active tuberculosis is that the tool used, principally the chest radiograph, results in large numbers of false positive results, incurring substantial human and capital cost.

Before supporting public health interventions through coercive measures policy makers need to show the effectiveness of a proposed intervention. And any benefits that might be accrued through the use of compulsion are certainly not grounded in evidence. Indeed what little evidence exists suggests that few migrants currently identified through screening abscond [hide themselves] that the introduction of compulsory measures may mean that some patients may delay seeking care and pose a greater public health threat.

Periodical Bibliography

The following articles have been selected to supplement the diverse views presented in this chapter.

Michael G. Baker and David P. Fidler — "Global Public Health Surveillance Under New International Health Regulations," *Emerging Infectious Diseases*, July 2006.

Jane Bradbury — "Beyond the Fire-Hazard Mentality of Medicine: The Ecology of Infectious Diseases," *PLoS Biology*, November 2003. http://biology.plos journals.org.

J. Gordon Edwards — "DDT: A Case Study in Scientific Fraud," *Journal of American Physicians and Surgeons*, Fall 2004.

Peter J. Hotez et al. — "A Global Fund to Fight Neglected Tropical Diseases: Is the G8 Hokkaido Toyako 2008 Summit Ready?" *PLoS Neglected Tropical Diseases*, March, 2008. www.plosntds.org.

Claudia Miller — "Mumps Resurgence Prompts Revised Recommendations," *Minnesota Medicine*, February, 2007. www.minnesotamedicine.com.

Roland Piquepaille — "Nanorobots to Improve Health Care," *ZDnet .com*, May 19, 2008. http://blogs.zdnet.com.

Leslie Roberts — "Resurgence of Yellow Fever in Africa Prompts a Counterattack," *Science*, May 25, 2007.

Elisabeth Rosenthal — "Case of TB Traveler Reveals Holes in Global Disease Control," *International Herald-Tribune*, May 31, 2007. www.iht.com.

Ameeta Eshri Singh et al. — "Resurgence of Early Congenital Syphilis in Alberta," *CMAJ*, July 3, 2007.

Rosanne Skirble — "Military Model Proposed to Combat Infectious Disease," *Voice of America*, March 10, 2006. www.voanews.com.

OPPOSING
VIEWPOINTS®
SERIES

CHAPTER 4

How Can Disease Resurgence Be Reduced?

Chapter Preface

Biochemist Mark Merchant and his colleagues are collecting alligator blood. It turns out that alligators are famous among scientists for their powerful immune systems. Despite the fact that alligators battle each other frequently and ferociously and live in microbe-laden swamps, their wounds heal without infection. In fact, an alligator's immune system can fight off fungi, viruses, and bacteria before ever having been exposed to them, unlike the human immune system, which must be infected before "learning" how to fight it. Merchant's team hopes to isolate the proteins behind this remarkable ability and adapt them for use in human medicine. Early research on alligator blood has already shown results in topical applications treating burned and ulcerated human skin.

All over the world, scientists are looking to the plant and animal kingdoms for new applications for existing substances, because the usual medicines used to kill the viruses, fungi, and bacteria that cause disease are starting to fail. Although antibiotics have been in widespread use for only about a hundred years, disease pathogens reproduce so quickly that they have experienced millions of generational cycles—plenty of time for those pathogens to evolve resistance to the treatments and cures available. Our medicines are failing, one after another, when human populations are mingling and sharing diseases like never before.

Fortunately, global interaction also provides opportunities for scientists from diverse nations to collaborate and share resources, as well as for scientists from distinct fields of study to provide new perspectives on old problems. For example, Australian biologists studying marsupials, which are born without immune systems and receive protection from secretions in the mothers' pouches, can partner with epidemiologists to solve immunodeficiencies in humans. Mathematicians and computer scientists can design software to model large-scale health management programs to evaluate options before implementation. Materials scientists and engineers are finding new ways to synthetically attack pathogens within the body and are developing new tools for distributing doses of medicines and preserving vaccines until they can reach remote populations.

Exciting innovation notwithstanding, discoveries and practical applications take many years to put into effect, since so many factors and contributors are involved. Alongside the scientists who find new treatments are public health management experts who devise ways to make the use of current drugs more effective and specific so pathogens have fewer opportunities to resist. At the global level, political leaders are making international agreements about drug use policy and drafting guidelines for health care workers to follow. At the local level, veterinarians are dropping some vaccines from pet health maintenance schedules (housecats who never go outside, for example, are less susceptible to infection) so that the vaccines are available for animals who are more at risk of contracting some diseases. In between are thousands of regional and national alliances of scientists and health care workers devising solutions to prevent the transmission of diseases in their own communities.

Reducing resistance to antibiotics and other drugs is just one way to reduce the resurgence of infectious diseases. The viewpoints in the following chapter explore some of the other routes being explored toward this end.

| *"Prevention of future [pertussis] outbreaks will likely rely on universal periodic vaccination of adolescents and adults."*

A Pertussis Booster Vaccine for Teens and Adults Is Needed to Prevent Future Outbreaks

Sean Schafer et al.

Sean Schafer is the Medical Monitoring Project director of the Oregon State Department of Human Services in the Office of Disease Prevention and Epidemiology. In the following viewpoint Schafer and his colleagues cite details of a 2003 outbreak of pertussis—whooping cough—in Oregon to contend that a general vaccine booster program for adolescents and adults would provide general immunity and lower infection rates.

Sean Schafer et al., "A Community-Wide Pertussis Outbreak: An Argument for Universal Booster Vaccination," *Archives of Internal Medicine*, vol. 166, no. 12, June 26, 2006, pp. 1317–1321.

As you read, consider the following questions:

1. According to the authors, in 2003, how did the rate of pertussis per one hundred thousand infants in Jackson County, Oregon, compare with the rate in the rest of the state?

2. What do Schafer et al. mean to say in the viewpoint that a one-month-old infant was the index case in a 2003 pertussis outbreak in Jackson County?

3. How would herd immunity ameliorate the difficulty of vaccinating some targeted groups against pertussis, in the authors' opinion?

Pertussis persists in the United States despite more than 50 years of routine childhood immunization against the disease. The reported incidence has increased steadily from 0.5 cases per 100,000 population in 1981 to an average annual rate of 3.3 cases per 100,000 population from 1996 through 2003. Although the incidence remains highest in incompletely immunized infants, the reported incidence has increased 5-fold among adolescents aged 10 to 19 years (from 0.3 to 7.7 per 100,000 population) and 4-fold among adults 20 years or older (from 0.3 to 1.1 per 100,000 population) from 1990 through 1993 to 2001 through 2003.

Pertussis among adolescents and adults has substantial direct consequences, being the likely cause of 12% to 30% of cases of prolonged cough. The true incidence has been estimated at 507 cases per 100,000 population, 150 times higher than reported, with resultant economic costs of $980 million annually in the United States. More important, adolescents and adults with pertussis frequently transmit infection to vulnerable infants, who experience more severe morbidity and nearly all pertussis-related mortality. Increased pertussis morbidity and mortality among US infants since the 1980s suggest that at least some of the recent rise in reported cases is real rather than solely an artifact of increased surveillance.

Large outbreaks have punctuated the resurgence of pertussis. These events often involve hundreds of cases and extend for many months. They tax public health resources and highlight the need for more effective means to interrupt transmission. We investigated one community-wide outbreak that lasted for most of 2003 in Jackson County, Oregon (2000 population, 181,269; county seat, Medford), to identify transmission patterns, risk factors for first-in-household adult infection, and opportunities for improved prevention and control. . . .

Jackson County Outbreak

During 2003, Jackson County reported 135 confirmed pertussis cases compared with 0 to 3 cases per year from 1995 through 2001. Countywide incidence was 71 per 100,000 population, and statewide incidence was 12.5 per 100,000. Jackson County incidence was 695.1 per 100,000 infants, 190.3 among children aged 1 to 4 years, 104.2 among children aged 5 to 9 years, 183.5 among those aged 10 to 17 years, and 38.6 among persons 18 years or older. Older children and teens aged 10 to 17 years accounted for 28% of all cases, and adults accounted for 39%. Five infants were hospitalized for pertussis in Jackson County in 2003 (192 hospitalized per 100,000 infants) compared with 18 in the remainder of the state (33 hospitalized per 100,000 infants). The state's single death from pertussis was outside Jackson County. A total of 2658 close contacts (19.7 per case) were identified through case investigation; 1050 (40%) of these were known to have received prescriptions for prophylactic antibiotics (erythromycin or azithromycin).

Routes of Transmission

In 2003, cases were reported in Jackson County from March through December, with notable peaks in May and late July through early August. We identified 2 groups of overlapping clusters of cases, both beginning in April. The first began with a cluster among an extended family, which spread to an elementary school classroom and a mail order supply company and eventually involved 20 cases.

The index case in the second group of overlapping clusters [see sidebar] was a 1-month-old infant living in a low-income apartment complex. Subsequently, 23 more cases were diagnosed during April and May among residents of the housing complex and their friends and relatives. These were linked to a cluster of cases among hotel housekeepers, 1 of whom babysat for the child with the index case. Several additional cases occurred in the household of another housekeeper and afterward in the elementary school of a child in this household. A second cluster was recognized in the elementary school classroom of a child with pertussis from the housing cluster of the index case.

In September, a new and apparently unrelated cluster of cases among inmates and deputies of the Jackson County jail was linked to methamphetamine users. When not incarcerated, these inmates lived in 3 adjacent "meth houses" across town from the housing complex cluster with approximately 20 other adults. Four additional adults among this group also had pertussis. Unexpectedly, the mother of the index case infant in the apartment complex cluster was recognized among these 4 adults. Having refused an offer of prophylaxis in the spring, she reported a prolonged cough in September. Although a nasopharyngeal culture result was negative, she had a confirmed pertussis case by virtue of clinical illness and an epidemiologic link to other laboratory-confirmed cases. Her diagnosis established a plausible route of transmission between springtime cases in the low-income apartment complex and summer and fall cases among jail inmates and methamphetamine users, and this enabled a total of 44 cases to be linked to this second group of epidemiologically linked clusters.

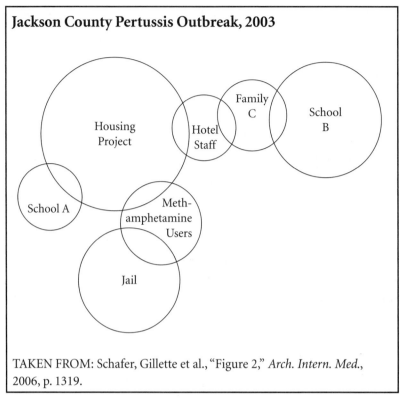

Jackson County Pertussis Outbreak, 2003

Housing Project

Hotel Staff

Family C

School B

School A

Meth-amphetamine Users

Jail

TAKEN FROM: Schafer, Gillette et al., "Figure 2," *Arch. Intern. Med.*, 2006, p. 1319.

Adult Infections

Among 53 adults with reported pertussis in Jackson County during 2003, the median age was 34 years (range, 18–55 years) and 32 (60%) were female; 28 (53%) had the first reported case in their household and were eligible for inclusion in the case-control study. Among these, 4 (14%) had laboratory-confirmed cases, 17 (61%) were female, and median age was 33 years (range, 18–55 years). We interviewed 20 (71%) of 28 eligible patients and 40 age- and sex-matched controls. The 40 controls were interviewed from 84 telephone numbers where an eligible person was clearly present (response rate, 48%). However, 40% of all randomly generated telephone numbers were unanswered after 3 or more tries or answered by a respondent who hung up before eligibility was determined.

Compared with controls, after stratified analysis, patients were more likely to live with children aged 6 to 10 years, less likely to report completion of college, less likely to have an income of $25,000 or more per year, and less likely to report having received all recommended childhood vaccinations (not necessarily limited to pertussis vaccines). In addition, they were more likely to smoke cigarettes. Factors not significantly associated with illness included institutional residence, illicit drug or alcohol use, air conditioning in the home, having asthma or other chronic illness, number of housemates, household crowding (persons per bedroom), reported vaccination status of household children, number of household children aged 2 to 5 years and 11 to 18 years, estimated daily personal contacts, and work with children. In multivariate analyses, patients remained 6.4 times as likely to live with children 6 to 10 years old and one tenth as likely to report having received all recommended childhood vaccinations (not restricted to pertussis-containing vaccines).

Curbing Infections

We investigated a community-wide pertussis outbreak, focusing on adult disease and tracing the progression of the outbreak across numerous distinct case clusters within the community. Several convergent lines of evidence argue that universal adolescent and adult pertussis booster vaccination offers the only effective means of preventing such events in the future. Most cases occurred among adolescents and adults, and although significantly fewer case patients than controls reported complete childhood vaccination, in our study most adult case patients (80%) reported having received a primary pertussis vaccination series. Current evidence indicates that *B pertussis* infection is many times higher than reported, meaning that most people with pertussis cannot be reached by a conventional, reactive "identify and prophylax" approach to interrupting transmission. This may be the reason that in our outbreak many new epidemiologically linked cases and clusters appeared despite aggressive treatment of reported cases and prophylaxis of contacts. Cases sometimes cluster in populations, such as the methamphetamine users in our outbreak, that public health nurses find difficult to reach. Such groups would likely be equally difficult to vaccinate if a targeted booster vaccination approach were to be attempted for control of future outbreaks. Achievement of significant herd immunity would reduce both the risk of introduction of disease into these hard-to-reach groups and secondary transmission to the broader community when such events occur. Apart from insufficient childhood immunization in a few, we found no specific, modifiable risk factors for first-in-household infection among adult cases that would allow for targeted prevention efforts. For these reasons, we agree with the Advisory Committee on Immunization Practices' recent recommendation of routine pertussis booster vaccination of adolescents and adults.

Most cases in this outbreak occurred among adolescents and adults. Several clusters included infants and children and specific instances of bidirectional transmission among children, adolescents, and adults. Clusters occurred in congregate settings where outbreaks have previously been reported, such as the workplace and schools, and other perhaps predictable but previously unreported settings, such as among methamphetamine users and jail inmates and employees. The number and diversity of settings in which clusters occurred suggest widespread adult susceptibility and abundant disease transmission when a case is coincidentally introduced into a congregate setting.

Until adolescent and adult booster vaccination became available, early identification and antibiotic treatment of cases as well as isolation and prophylaxis of at-risk contacts were the only available methods of preventing secondary cases and interrupting outbreaks. Evidence from other studies that only a minority of pertussis cases are recognized suggests that this traditional approach has, at best, modest impact. In this outbreak, despite aggressive application of these conventional control methods, new cases and clusters continued to occur, often in congregate settings where successful antibiotic treatment and prophylaxis could be thwarted by cost, limited health care access, and chaotic or impoverished lifestyles (eg, jails, crowded housing, or communities of illicit drug users). Similar barriers hinder vaccination of exposed children. In addition, isolating exposed contacts in such settings is often impractical. Consequently, prolonged transmission within and between focal clusters persists.

Children's Infection Risk

Our case-control study attempted to identify specific characteristics of adults at greatest risk who might be targeted for prevention or control efforts, such as intensified contact tracing and treatment or booster vaccination. However, we identified only 2 significant, independent risk factors: having school-aged children in the household and incomplete childhood vaccination. Although we limited enrollment of cases to adults whose infection was thought to be primary within their household, we suspect that school-aged children in the home—many with immunity beginning to wane from earlier vaccination—might acquire subclinical cases of pertussis and transmit infection to household adults who lack natural immunity and have even less residual vaccine-induced protection than their children. Consistent with this scenario, one previous study found the presence of adolescents in a household to be associated with reported infection, another study found that primary cases were most frequent among children in household clusters, and a more recent study found that household composition, including the presence of children aged 6 to 11 years, was associated with pertussis in preschoolers. Insufficient immunity is the obvious explanation for the association between incomplete childhood vaccination and infection. However, 16 of 20 patients in our study had been fully immunized, substantiating the influence of waning immunity.

Our investigation has several limitations. First, reported cases are not likely to be representative of all cases. Milder cases, sporadic cases, and those occurring in adults or other persons with a comorbid cough illness or limited access to care are probably underrepresented among reported cases. Second, ascertainment bias is a possible alternative explanation for observed associations in a case-control study. A child who has pertussis after an initially undetected primary adult case in a household might have the condition diagnosed more readily, leading to belated recognition of the antecedent adult case. Third, recall bias might have contributed to the observed association between case status and incomplete childhood vaccination. Finally, a low response rate (48%) threatens the interpretation of our case-control study of adult risks. A random digit-dialing approach permitted us to reach and interview controls through methods comparable to those used for cases (eg, home telephones, cellular telephones, businesses, and institutions such as jails and dormitories), perhaps at the cost of a more desirable response rate.

After approval by the Food and Drug Administration and recent demonstration of 92% vaccine efficacy among adults, booster vaccination of adolescents and adults has been recommended by the Advisory Committee on Immunization Practices. An economic analysis estimated that vaccination of adolescents might save $1.6 billion a year. Although our investigation suggests that adults and adolescents with incomplete or unrecollected childhood vaccination histories and those with school-aged children in the home might be ushered to the front of the booster vaccination line, prevention of future outbreaks will likely rely on universal periodic vaccination of adolescents and adults, with limited roles for more targeted approaches.

> *"Lack of communication and universal cooperation with providers at the local level may have contributed to the extent of this [pertussis] outbreak."*

Preventing Pertussis Outbreaks Requires Improved Public Health Management

J. Gary Wheeler et al.

J. Gary Wheeler is professor of pediatrics in the Section of Infectious Diseases at the University of Arkansas for Medical Sciences; his coauthors are associated with the university and the state health department. In the following viewpoint, the authors note the failure of the public health system to curtail and manage an outbreak of pertussis (whooping cough) in Arkansas and maintain that improvements in efficiency and communication at the public health system level are necessary to avoid future outbreaks.

J. Gary Wheeler et al., "Barriers to Public Health Management of a Pertussis Outbreak in Arkansas," *Archives of Pediatric and Adolescent Medicine*, vol. 158, no. 2, February 2004, pp. 146–152. Copyright © 2004 American Medical Association. All rights reserved. Reproduced by permission.

As you read, consider the following questions:

1. What national health emergency interfered with the Center for Disease Control and Prevention's involvement in the 2001 Arkansas pertussis outbreak, as reported by the authors?

2. Why did previously accurate diagnostic tests fail to be of use during the Arkansas pertussis outbreak, according to Wheeler et al.?

3. In the authors' opinion, what was the relationship between the citizenry's trust in public health services and the extent of the pertussis outbreak?

Each fall, the number of pertussis cases increases in Arkansas. In August 2001, the first cases indicating the onset of the respiratory season were noted. On September 28, 2001, a physician in "county A" telephoned the ACH [Arkansas Children's Hospital] to report a few suspected cases of pertussis in his town. While attending a junior high school football game the night before, he noticed many of the players going to the sidelines after each play with coughing and subsequent emesis [vomiting]. The day of this report, the ACH called the local health unit of county A, ADH [Arkansas Department of Health] contacted the CDC [Centers for Disease Control and Prevention], and local health nurses went to the school and began the investigation; 15 students were sent home. The next day, ADH communicable disease nurses began investigating the outbreak, and 50 to 100 students were sent home. The county health officer (a physician) was instructed to ensure that all physicians in his county were aware of the outbreak. Students identified as cases were excluded from school until 5 days of prophylaxis was completed. Contacts with no symptoms were not excluded but were given prophylaxis. The school closed for 3 days owing to lack of attendance.

It was clear that a larger-than-usual outbreak was occurring statewide. On October 5, 2001, a press release was issued, a story appeared in the local media, and the ADH notified health care providers in the state via fax and e-mail. However, the day before the scheduled press release (October 4), anthrax reports appeared, and the CDC began focusing primarily on controlling anthrax. On October 10, the ACH microbiology laboratory contacted the CDC medical epidemiology unit.

The next day, the ADH began sending pertussis newsletters to hospital administrators and chiefs of staff with instructions to distribute the newsletter to all physicians on staff. No verification process existed to guarantee the delivery of these messages. At this point, there were 88 cases of pertussis in county A and confirmed cases in 5 other counties. The county health officer in each county with increased numbers of cases was notified.

On October 16, 2001, county A reported its last case. Cooperation was good among local physicians, school officials, the CDC, public health nurses, and families during the outbreak, which lasted a little more than 2 months. There were 116 cases in a population of 11,303.

At the end of October 2001, "county B" reported suspected cases of pertussis. It was reported by field nurses that suggestions for prophylaxis and isolation of cases by the local health unit were implemented less successfully in county B than in county A. It is unclear whether this was due to poor provider recognition, less effective communications, community attitudes, or other issues.

Managing the Outbreak

The infectious disease service of the Department of Pediatrics at the University of Arkansas for Medical Sciences provided telephone consultation for medical practices in Arkansas regarding children's infectious diseases. During the peak October period, they received 5 to 15 questions per day from local health care providers concerning pertussis management.

Between December 1, 2001, and February 28, 2002, the ACH (located in county C) admitted 50 patients with positive laboratory results (including direct fluorescent antibody [DFA]) suggesting pertussis infection. In previous years, the hospital averaged 2 to 3 admissions with positive laboratory results per month. Between July 1, 2001, and June 30, 2002, 113 hospital employee pertussis exposures required prophylaxis. For the similar period in 2000–2001, there were less than 20 exposures and only 4 employees with symptoms and a positive DFA test result.

By the middle of October 2001, the ACH laboratory was receiving 30 to 40 culture swabs per day from clinicians, exceeding the laboratory's capacity to process specimens. The ACH microbiology laboratory communicated with officials from the CDC respiratory disease branch several times to discuss pertussis culture, PCR [polymerase chain reaction], and methods for DNA collection and isolation. These communications were primarily via e-mail because telephone access to the CDC was difficult during the anthrax crisis. The laboratory requested media that was not available from distributors from the CDC, and it was provided within a week.

Diagnostic Procedures

The ACH laboratory stopped culturing for pertussis on February 20, 2002, and PCR became the routine method for pertussis testing on May 28, 2002. Because of the heightened community anxiety present about pertussis, increased numbers of patients were requesting therapy. Many referring physicians relied on DFA test results for treatment decisions, whether the patient had symptoms or fit the case definition or not. This occurred even as the reliability of the DFA test was being challenged.

By November 21, 2001, more than 400 cases of pertussis were confirmed by culture or case definition in Arkansas, and cases of pertussis had been found in 34 of the state's 75 counties.

NCR Disease Surveillance Network

The NCR [National Capital Region] network uses the Electronic Surveillance System for the Early Notification of Community-based Epidemics (ESSENCE), developed by the [Johns Hopkins University Applied Physics] Lab with the Walter Reed Army Institute of Research. ESSENCE compiles data containing health indicators, performs analysis and provides information to local and regional public health officials on statistical anomalies that occur to help them identify bio-events early. Such irregularities would include upward trends in rashes, fevers and unexplained deaths, or a sudden surge in over-the-counter drug sales. It is the first system to integrate military and civilian data.

Each local and state public health jurisdiction in the NCR network responds independently to public health alerts and to ensure the health and safety of its residents. With an unprecedented collaborative network among public health programs, the NCR disease surveillance system offers a first line of defense in the national capital area.

Johns Hopkins University Applied Physics
Laboratory press release, April 27, 2005. www.jhuapl.edu.

The number of cases peaked in October 2001, but the outbreak continued until June 2002. The ACH laboratory, received 3442 samples between September 1, 2001, and April 30, 2002. The total number of cases was approximately 10-fold the number reported in any of the past 10 years. No deaths were caused by pertussis based on review of the ADH vital statistics. . . .

Diagnostic Breakdown

One of the first problems encountered was difficulty in diagnosis. Although pertussis is well described and case definitions have existed for years, determination of a case is anything but precise. Since pertussis disease is based on a clinical definition, diagnosis is based on perceptions and observations of the parent or patient who reports the symptoms and on the physician who determines the diagnosis. Failure to consider the diagnosis of pertussis in children was described in Canada, where only one fourth of the children who met the case definition were considered to have pertussis. Pertussis-like disease is clearly mimicked by other pathogens and processes that produce respiratory symptoms and repetitive coughing. Only 33% of submitted samples from suspected cases were positive by any method. In a [national emergency], individuals with similar symptoms as the case definition would imagine that their symptoms resemble those of the case definition, as occurred at ACH among personnel and among communities seeking a diagnosis of and therapy for pertussis. Similar behaviors were noted in Arkansas during the reporting of cases of anthrax nationally, although no cases were diagnosed in this state.

Ideally, some definitive testing procedures would be available. In this outbreak, tests (DFA) previously considered effective by local authorities ultimately failed. For years, the DFA test under rigid conditions and trained eyes had reasonable specificity and sensitivity. Under the stress of large numbers of samples, however, its sensitivity and specificity waned as tired or less trained eyes were called on to review these subjective test results. During [an epidemic] technicians would be taxed with large numbers of clinical samples. It seems reasonable to have trained non-public health technicians in reserve, much like the armed forces are backed up by reserves. Equipment would also need to be updated to provide adequate support for the technical reserves as well. In Arkansas, a private children's hospital (ACH) fulfilled this reserve support, but as the only laboratory in the state providing pertussis diagnosis, its effectiveness ultimately lessened.

Another issue was the problem of implementing new diagnostic testing (PCR). The AHD was in transition and had funding issues that marginalized their microbiology laboratory and epidemiology services, and the ACH ultimately chose to set up PCR diagnostics. Providing adequate molecular laboratories in all state health departments with common technical support through the CDC or other central laboratory would avoid this obstacle. Material support needs to be coordinated as well, since media was in short supply for bacterial cultures in this outbreak and one could well imagine shortages of other reagents for any testing method. Another issue, not a factor in this outbreak, is the determination of antimicrobial sensitivity. [For example,] bioterrorist-released microbes may be engineered to be drug resistant. If so, central laboratories for testing must be available. To make such a system work, efficient transportation of samples would be required as well. Currently in Arkansas, an informal courier system exists that randomly delivers samples for diagnosis. Some samples in our outbreak arrived by mail, a process forbidden by federal law. Systematic specimen transport is required and should be planned. We believe that the lack of rapid and precise diagnosis played a major role in early recognition and containment of this epidemic.

Vaccine Availability

The classic approach to disease prevention is vaccination. Among the most important lessons is the vulnerability of our vaccine supply. In some cases, vaccines are prepared by only 1 or 2 manufacturers. Although the pertussis vaccine was made by 4 manufacturers at the beginning of the outbreak, the cessation of production by 2 manufacturers for business reasons led to a shortfall in production that reduced vaccine availability at the worst possible time during this outbreak. Health care providers provided the minimal amount of protection with available resources, and they did so with maximal effort and considerable disturbance in the office routine. Patients were recalled later for catch-up vaccinations when the vaccine supply was reestablished, and much explanation to confused parents was required. Clearly, protection of the vaccine supply is critical in future protection against preventable diseases.

Questions were considered regarding the efficacy of the new DTaP [diptheria, tetanus, and acellular pertussis] vaccine. However, most of the affected children in this outbreak were older and were vaccinated with the whole-cell diphtheria, tetanus, pertussis toxoid (DTP) vaccine. The observation of a shift in disease rates to older children and adults has been well described. Therefore, we do not believe that vaccination status was a factor in this outbreak. . . .

Public Health Management

Based on our review, the ADH and CDC staff responded quickly with specific plans once an epidemic was recognized. However, a rapid systematic response to an infectious disease outbreak was not achieved from disease surveillance but by the fortunate observations of a single clinician. Communications with local providers were recognized to be hit or miss, and there was no clear and dependable way to reach every health care worker. In addition, communications with the CDC were difficult and were fully dependent on e-mail. One could draw the conclusion that an appropriate step in the future for state health departments would be to require an e-mail, fax, or other electronic communications network for health care providers and municipal leaders. This network would correspond to civil defense networks and allow instant communications. Still, vulnerability in this plan would be the Internet itself, which can be targeted for computer viruses, "spamming," or other attacks. . . .

At the state level, additional lessons were learned. The reorganization of the ADH left the department less able to quickly respond to some of the needs during the pertussis outbreak. Departments will always need overhauls. During these reorganizations, clear policy and leadership to address infectious and ecologic disasters should be left intact.

The infrastructure of the ADH was also hindered by the transition to a new computing system. Case identification in the field by hand is no longer appropriate, and the state departments should rapidly correct computer infrastructural problems that will allow in-the-field computing and immediate data entry and analysis. This should be a federal and state priority. Finally, health departments need adequate budgets to succeed in their mission to protect the public health. Federal support needs to be present if states individually cannot provide this revenue. Implicit in these budgetary issues is the relationship of the state health department, the state citizenry, and the legislature that funds the department. Building public relations is critical in preparation for a crisis. The public must trust the health department and follow its instructions to successfully combat an outbreak. In Arkansas, this was suggested by the response in county A, where cooperation was high and the outbreak was quickly eliminated, vs county B, where trust and cooperation were reported to be low and the outbreak continued for months. Federal and state health departments must strive for excellence and must be quickly responsive to their customers (citizens and health providers) to garner trust. The trust must be built during times of noncrisis. This tension is not new to this epidemic but has existed throughout the history of public health departments in this country. We believe that lack of communication and universal cooperation with providers at the local level may have contributed to the extent of this outbreak. In addition, physicians must be trained to accept responsibility and partnerships as part of the public health team.

"No valid reason exists to retain small-pox virus stocks."

The Smallpox Virus Should Be Completely Destroyed

Edward Hammond

Edward Hammond is the director of the United States Office of the Sunshine Project, an organization dedicated to strengthening the global consensus against biological warfare and preventing the development and use of biological weapons. In the following viewpoint, Hammond argues that since smallpox was eradicated from the human population in 1980, the strains of the virus that still exist in labs in the United States and Russia should be completely destroyed as there is no valid reason for keeping them around and their destruction would ensure that no future outbreak occurs.

As you read, consider the following questions:

1. When was the genome of the *Variola* virus sequenced in the United States, according to Hammond?

2. Why is it unnecessary to preserve smallpox virus stocks against a future bioterrorism attack, in the author's opinion?

Edward Hammond, "Should the U.S. and Russia Destroy Their Stocks of Smallpox Virus?" *British Medical Journal*, vol. 334, no. 7597, April 14, 2007, p. 774. Copyright © 2007 British Medical Association. Reproduced by permission.

3. Where did the smallpox virus samples stockpiled in the United States and Russia come from, according to Hammond?

The World Health Organization [WHO] is justly proud of the global effort that led to the eradication of smallpox; but the truth is that the job remains unfinished. Although it is almost 30 years since the last natural transmission of smallpox virus (*Variola*), laboratories in the United States and Russia retain virus stocks.

The destruction of remaining *Variola* stocks is an overdue step forward for global public health and security that will greatly reduce the possibility that this scourge will kill again, by accident or design. Although deploying modern scientific techniques such as genetic engineering on smallpox virus may be intellectually intriguing, the risks far outweigh the potential benefits.

Pledges to Destroy Smallpox

In 1990, the US secretary of health and human services, Louis Sullivan, made a pledge on behalf of the US government. "There is no scientific reason not to destroy the remaining stocks of wild virus," he declared, "So I am pleased to announce today that after we complete our sequencing of the smallpox genome, the United States will destroy all remaining virus stocks." Although the genome was published in 1994, the US still hasn't honoured its commitment.

WHO member states concur that the virus stocks must be destroyed. For more than a decade, the US and Russia have paid lip service to the WHO consensus while trying to outmanoeuvre actual destruction of the virus. In 1999 Russia and the US balked at the World Health Assembly resolution calling on them to destroy the virus. Since then, both countries have accelerated smallpox research. Particularly risky experiments are underway to create a monkey model of human smallpox infection. The US has also proposed genetic engineering experiments with the virus.

Stockpiling Brings No Benefits

WHO's experts have agreed that no valid reason exists to retain smallpox virus stocks for DNA sequencing, diagnostic tests, or vaccine development. In 2006, WHO's experts concluded: "Sufficient sequence information on the virus was now available; no further research requiring access to live variola virus was considered essential." They also determined that "the number of detection and diagnostic systems for variola virus now available was adequate." Antivirals are not absolutely required because existing vaccines are effective and diagnostic tests are rapid and accurate. And WHO experts have recently suggested that drugs against smallpox could be developed without the dangerous US experiments with live smallpox virus intended to create an animal model of human infection. WHO advisers suggest that this could be accomplished through the far safer route of using monkeypox virus.

A Questionable Threat

The US has recently made much of the possibility of smallpox in the hands of terrorists or "rogue states." Illicit stocks have been used to justify retention of US and Russian smallpox virus stocks. There is a fallacy lurking here because smallpox virus stocks are not necessary to respond to a smallpox outbreak. If smallpox reappeared, the virus would be readily available if needed for biomedical purposes.

The claims about illicit stocks have also not been supported by evidence. The loudest allegations were against Iraq, but the US belatedly admitted that it was wrong. There is no credible evidence that any terrorist organisation has smallpox virus. To acquire the virus terrorists would have to breach se-

Specicide

Given how hard we try to prevent the demise of one species or another—from the African elephant to the northern hairy-nosed wombat—it may seem perverse to entertain the notion of causing an extinction on purpose. Yet there's a handful of species we've tried (and failed) to destroy—at great expense, both to the environment and to our wallets. Chief among these, and the most obvious candidate for specicide, is the *Anopheles* mosquito, the mosquito that spreads malaria. . . .

The earth is home to more than 2,500 species of mosquito. Even if we were to eradicate the approximately 30 species that are regular carriers of malaria, and for good measure, the *Aedes* mosquitoes that spread dengue and yellow fever, we'd hardly be creating a mosquito-free world. It is hard to argue that a targeted, genetic attempt to remove an insect that is clearly harmful to us is worse than the haphazard, expensive, destructive and largely unsuccessful approach we're using now.

Olivia Judson, New York Times, *September 25, 2003.*

curity at one of WHO's repositories. Producing quantities of weaponised smallpox is beyond the means of any known terrorist group.

Increasing Danger

The US National Science Advisory Board on Biosecurity is currently discussing a proposal to weaken domestic legislation to permit US laboratories to synthesise and possess larger sequences of smallpox DNA. This will make its DNA easier to acquire and increase the range of dangerous experiments possible outside the official WHO virus repositories.

In 2005, the head of the WHO eradication effort, Donald Henderson, told the [London] *Independent*: "The less we do with the smallpox virus and the less we do in the way of manipulation at this point I think the better off we are." Yet one unfortunate consequence of the US insistence that its smallpox virus is critical to its national security is that other countries may become convinced that they too must possess the virus and research into it. The smallpox strains in the WHO repositories in the US and Russia were deposited by various countries and were isolated all over the world. It is extremely unclear who legally owns the collections.

The decades-old eradication job of WHO will be completed, and the world will be safer, when the US and Russian smallpox virus stocks are finally destroyed. Recently, Africa has taken the lead at the World Health Assembly. Its health ministers see all too clearly what could happen if smallpox were to escape. Africa's efforts, with support from other developing regions, have put WHO member states into a position to do more than recall unfulfilled pledges when the World Health Assembly convenes in May 2007.

As memory of the horror of smallpox recedes and biotechnology advances, it is important to draw a firm line around *Variola*. Instead of courting disaster, we should seek to ensure that possession of this virus is treated as a crime against humanity. The key prerequisite to criminalising *Variola* is to destroy the existing stocks. It has been three decades coming, but it is time for WHO to push the button on the autoclave [a steam-heated device used for sterilization]. Better late than too late.

"*According to the World Health Organization, doctors are estimated to over-prescribe antibiotics by 50 percent.*"

Better Drug Management Will Thwart Bacterial Resistance

Judy Monroe

The following viewpoint explains how bacteria develops resistance to antibiotics and makes recommendations for slowing this process. The author discusses how antibiotics have become less effective because of over-prescription, demand for antibiotics when not appropriate, and failure to finish an antibiotic treatment. The viewpoint also provides a list of appropriate steps to take to limit the development of antibiotic resistance, such as getting recommended vaccines when traveling outside of the United States. Judy Monroe is a freelance writer for Current Health 2, a Weekly Reader Publication.

As you read, consider the following questions:

1. When did antibiotics first become available as a treatment for infectious diseases?

2. According to the viewpoint, what are four factors that contribute to antibiotic resistance?

3. List three steps you can take to limit the development of antibiotic resistance, according to the viewpoint.

When introduced in the 1940s, antibiotics were touted as miracle drugs. Are they still miracle drugs—or have they lost their healing power?

In 1995, a 16-year-old had a fever, diarrhea, and stomach cramps. Doctors suspected he had a bacterial infection, so they gave him the usual antibiotic treatments. But he didn't get better until he received the help of another antibiotic.

Unfortunately, this has not been the only case of bacterial resistance to antibiotics. Many other infectious germs now outwit some of the most commonly used antibiotics. Some of these bacteria cause pneumonia, ear infections, acne, gonorrhea, urinary tract infections, salmonella and tuberculosis. According to the Mayo Clinic in Rochester, Minnesota, drug reliance may have contributed to the 58 percent rise in infectious disease deaths among Americans between 1980 and 1992.

Increasing Antibiotic Resistance

Antibiotics have been the foundation of infectious disease treatment since the first penicillin became available in the early 1940s. Since then, dozens of other antibiotics have been developed.

Antibiotics have remarkable healing powers against bacterial infections. They work by either killing bacteria or by inhibiting their growth. However, they have no effect on viral infections such as the common cold or flu.

Soon after penicillin and other antibiotics were discovered, antibiotic-resistant bacteria began to emerge. Antibiotic resistance continues to increase.

"We've reached a situation where it's no longer an isolated problem of this bug or that bug," says a spokesperson for the U.S. Centers for Disease Control and Prevention (CDC). "Virtually all important human pathogens treatable with antibiotics have developed some resistance." So, infections once treatable by common antibiotics have become resistant to those specific drugs. These antibiotics, therefore, no longer work on that bacteria.

Take salmonella, a bacterial infection. In the United States, egg-associated outbreaks of salmonella hit during the 1990s. The bacteria can be inside normal-looking eggs. If the eggs are eaten raw or undercooked, the bacteria can cause illness, with stomach cramps, fever, and diarrhea. The illness usually lasts four to seven days. In 1999, there were 44 outbreaks of this infection reported to the CDC.

The total number of salmonella outbreaks reported in 1999 was similar to those in 1998. However, the CDC saw something different from these statistics: There were about twice as many illnesses. This may have been due to antibiotic resistance.

Another example is tuberculosis, a chronic bacterial infection that affects the lungs. It causes more deaths worldwide than any other infectious disease. Antibiotics often cure tuberculosis. In recent years, however, drug-resistant cases have increased.

Contributing Factors

Health experts list four factors that contribute to antibiotic resistance:

- Misuse and/or overuse of antibiotics in people, animals, and agriculture. According to the World Health Organization, doctors are estimated to overprescribe antibiotics by 50 percent.

- Demand for antibiotics when these drugs are not appropriate. Sometimes people request an antibiotic to treat a viral infection. Antibiotics don't work on viruses.

It was on a short-cut through the hospital kitchens that Albert was first approached by a member of the Antibiotic Resistance.

Cartoon by Nick D. Kim, nearingzero.net, used by permission.

- Failure to finish an antibiotic treatment. In underdeveloped countries, some people can't afford to buy the antibiotics to treat the infection.

- Availability of antibiotics without a prescription in some countries.

Bacterial Resistance

Bacteria are living microbes able to mutate, or change themselves. They also acquire resistant genes from other microbes. They do this to develop reliance to existing antibiotic drugs.

Actually, antibiotic resistance is a natural process. When bacteria are exposed to an antibiotic, the weaker ones die. The resistant or stronger bacteria remain. Through this selective process, resistant bacteria become the norm. Such a bacterial infection can outwit all antibiotics.

These are frightening trends. However, most people aren't likely to run into a superbug, says the U.S. Food and Drug Administration (FDA). Though the risk of this happening remains low, it's important to know which bugs are prevalent in which areas.

What happens is that doctors are forced to rely on drugs that are more costly and possibly toxic to some people. So a sick person may have to take a series of antibiotics rather than just one.

Many health experts are concerned by the recent, rapid increase in antibiotic resistance and expect the problem to worsen.

Combating Bacterial Resistance to Antibiotics

As long as antibiotics are used, drug resistance will remain a challenge. The U.S. Department of Health and Human Services (HHS) recently unveiled a four-part action plan to combat this problem:

1. Surveillance. The CDC is working with national, state, and other health organizations to define and coordinate surveillance responsibilities. Data collected will provide early warnings of outbreaks, identify changing resistance patterns, guide drug development, and target prevention measures. Also, departments plan to monitor patterns of antibiotic use in human medicine, agriculture, and consumer products.

2. Prevention and Control. The HHS and others are launching a national public education campaign to reduce the overuse and misuse of antibiotics. The CDC has already started to prepare guidelines for health professionals on how best to use antibiotics.

3. Research. The HHS is leading a team of agencies that will look at new information and technologies to de-

velop new treatments to prevent new infections from forming and stop the spread of resistant bacteria.

4. Product Development. A new group will identify and publicize priority health needs for new products that prevent resistance or treat resistant infections.

Superbugs are not an everyday problem for most of us. Hopefully, they'll remain that way.

Limiting Development of Antibiotic Resistance

You can help to limit the development of antibiotic resistance. Here are some steps to take:

1. Don't demand antibiotics from your doctor. If you are given antibiotics for a bacterial infection, take them exactly as prescribed. Don't stop because you're feeling better, and don't share your medicine with anyone else.

2. Be aware of food-poisoning bacteria.

   - Antibiotics are often used in agriculture. So, wash fruits and vegetables well.

   - Don't eat raw eggs and undercooked meat. Most foods that cause disease are raw or undercooked foods of animal origin such as meat, milk, eggs, cheese, fish, or shellfish.

   - Keep perishable foods such as meat, milk, eggs, fish, or shellfish refrigerated. Don't eat any of these if they have been at room temperature for over two hours.

   - Discard cracked or dirty eggs.

   - Wash your hands, cooking utensils, pots, and pans with soap and hot water after contact with raw, perishable foods.

- Avoid restaurant dishes made with raw or under-cooked, unpasteurized eggs. If restaurants serve items like hollandaise sauce or Caesar salad dressing, for example, check that they use pasteurized eggs.

3. Wash your hands after using the toilet.

4. If you travel outside the United States, get the recommended vaccines. Check with your doctor. Some underdeveloped countries, for example, may have food and water contaminated with salmonella.

Periodical Bibliography

The following articles have been selected to supplement the diverse views presented in this chapter.

Kristy Barnes — "New Vaccine Technology Holds Double Promise," *PharmaTechnologist.com*, March 5, 2007.

Peter Dunn — "Research Could Put Penicillin Back in Battle Against Antibiotic Resistant Bugs That Kill Millions," University of Warwick, March 10, 2008. www.warwick.ac.uk.

Scott Fields — "New Approach Disarms Deadly Bacteria," *LiveScience*, December 29, 2006. www.live science.com.

Andrea Gawrylewski — "MRSA: RIP?" *TheScientist.com*, December 11, 2007. www.the-scientist.com.

Danielle Jacobs — "The Bug Zappers," *Endeavors* (University of North Carolina), Winter 2008.

Fred Pearce — "Africa's Cassava Comeback," *New Scientist*, April 19, 2007.

Jorge Salazar — "Rita Colwell on Disease and Climate," *Earth & Sky*, March 13, 2008. www.earthsky.org.

Harvey B. Simon — "Old Bugs Learn Some New Tricks: As More Drugs Are Created to Fight Infection, Bacteria Mutate and Strike in Another Form," *Newsweek*, December 11, 2006.

Nikhil Swaminathan — "Bacterial Bait and Switch: Germs Tricked into Absorbing Wrong Element," *Scientific American*, March 19, 2007. www.sciam.com

TerraDaily — "Climate and Cholera," April 2, 2008. www.terradaily.com.

Marlene Zuk — "Drug Resistance, Explained," *New York Times*, March 27, 2008.

For Further Discussion

Chapter 1

1. James L. Dickerson warns that global warming could unleash warm-weather pathogens into formerly cold-weather environments that are not prepared for them. Paul Reiter's research team argues that human technology and lifestyle can ward off diseases whether global warming triggers outbreaks or not. Should any resources currently allocated to fighting and preventing diseases be diverted to climate study and global warming prevention? How could either a yes or no answer be justified?

2. Progress for disease treatment and containment is often hampered by unanticipated events or unexpected opinions. If catastrophes such as war or phenomena such as mass vaccination rejection occur in one country or region, how can neighboring nations or surrounding regions protect themselves against infections that are not being controlled? Do you think quarantines at the global level are likely to work? Why or why not?

Chapter 2

1. Sabin Russell argues that MRSA is a very dangerous infection that is difficult to treat in the best circumstances and can be spread through populations. Jim Burroway protests Russell's claim that gay people are responsible for its presence, but points his finger at athletes. Should the public be informed when diseases like MRSA appear in certain groups? There is a possibility that the smaller group will be scapegoated by the larger group. But does the danger of contagion, caused by ignorance and the resulting inability to take precautions against the infection, outweigh the social risk? Explain your answer, citing from the viewpoints.

180

2. Amy Goodman's interview with Robert Daniels portrays him as a person with an illness who did not believe he was endangering other people. Fidler, Gostin, and Markel, meanwhile, claim that it is reasonable to isolate individuals who may harm others by infecting them with disease. Should people be punished for exposing others to infection out of ignorance? Out of neglect? Knowingly? Why or why not?

3. Currently, disease research and management is conducted by government and private organizations worldwide. Government often has the advantage of a far reach and institutional stability; private enterprise often has the advantage of targeted projects and rapid access to money and supplies. If either government or private funding were to disappear completely, which source would you want to remain? Explain why you think this source can be more successful.

Chapter 3

1. As Paul K. Driessen reports, DDT has been banned by many countries as an environmental hazard, despite weak evidence that it harms animals and strong evidence that it helps humans. Some countries in Europe have even gone so far as to threaten trade sanctions against other countries that use DDT. Does one country have the right to make demands about how another country treats its environment? Is the global environment more important than the health of individual people? Is a government that decides to use DDT to combat malaria, thereby limiting its own economic opportunities, harming or helping its people in the long run? Explain your answer, citing from the viewpoints.

2. To varying degrees, both Lorenz von Seidlein and G. Balakrish Nair blame the presence of cholera in India on government inaction. The government of India is large, but it

is responsible for a billion people—a population of staggering size—and cannot achieve all of its public health goals simultaneously. If you could make the decision, would you prioritize distributing vaccines above providing clean water and sanitation systems? What benefits might accompany either course of action? What harms?

3. Richard Coker argues that the general screening for tuberculosis of all immigrants to the United Kingdom is unwarranted and unethical. Penny Brewin's research group found that general screening is appropriate and that most immigrants are happy to be tested. Does the willingness of immigrants to undergo this test absolve potential ethical problems? Does the fact that tuberculosis is relatively noncontagious justify the financial cost of screening all those people? How would your answers change if all immigrants were to be screened for other diseases?

Chapter 4

1. As J. Gary Wheeler's research team discovered, unforeseen events or government priority levels can significantly affect public health efforts (positively or negatively) to stem disease outbreaks. Sean Schafer's research team made clear, however, that diseases are transmitted from one person to another; ultimately, the management of a disease is left up to a doctor and a patient. To what extent should doctors and patients rely on public health measures to protect themselves from disease outbreaks? Would money that is currently used for public health reactions to disease outbreaks be better spent on public awareness campaigns? Is disease management a social or a personal issue? Defend your answers, citing from the viewpoints.

2. The overuse of antibiotics and the bacterial adaptation of drug resistance have given doctors fewer choices with which to fight disease. Paradoxically, the small numbers of remaining medical drugs means that health care work-

ers will be using them in far greater numbers than before, which could possibly speed up the process of pathogens becoming resistant to them. Considering that people still get sick and require prompt treatment, how can doctors and patients—not researchers and drug developers—approach the problem of limiting drug overuse while still aggressively treating disease in individuals and outbreaks within communities?

3. The status of a virus as a life form is debatable: viruses do not have DNA (they rely on RNA), and they cannot reproduce without other cells. One aspect of the controversy surrounding the proposed incineration of the remaining stocks of the smallpox virus is whether or not humans have the right to deliberately make extinct another species. Does the human species have the right to protect itself against a virus species that kills a third of the people it infects? Is total obliteration an appropriate response? Would the conscious obliteration of a virus species be likely to become a habit of obliterating other species that humans consider dangerous? Explain your answers, citing from the viewpoints.

Organizations to Contact

Centers for Disease Control and Prevention (CDC)
1600 Clifton Rd., Atlanta, GA   30333
(404) 498-1515
Web site: www.cdc.gov

The CDC is one of the major components of the United States Department of Health and Human Services. Its mission is to promote health and quality of life by preventing and controlling disease, injury, and disability. It works with partner agencies around the world to monitor health, detect and investigate health problems, conduct research to enhance prevention, develop and advocate sound public health policies, implement prevention strategies, promote healthy behaviors, foster safe and healthful environments, and provide leadership and training to health workers and communities. It publishes many reports and journals, including *Emerging Infectious Diseases*, and past and current issues are available on the Web site.

Centers for Law and the Public's Health
624 N. Broadway, Hampton House, Room 588
Baltimore, MD   21205-1996
(410) 955-7624 • fax: (410) 614-9055
Web site: www.publichealthlaw.net

The Centers for Law and the Public's Health are primary, international, national, state, and local resources on public health law, ethics, and policy for public health practitioners, lawyers, legislators, judges, academics, policymakers, and others. They are a collaboration of Johns Hopkins and Georgetown Universities. Their mission is to improve understanding about how the law affects the prevention of disease and injury through research, education, training, collaboration, and dissemination of information and to promote the development and implementation of an effective public health law infrastructure.

Their staff and faculty teach courses and conduct research on public health and legal topics. The centers' project reports and policy proposals are available on their Web site.

Global Health Council

1111 Nineteenth St. NW #1120, Washington, DC 20036
(202) 833-5900 • fax: (202) 833-0075
Web site: www.globalhealth.org

The Global Health Council is an alliance of health care professionals, organizations, philanthropic foundations, and government agencies dedicated to improving health around the world. It informs and educates leaders, policy makers, media representatives, and citizens about crucial global health issues. It generates public awareness via television, newspaper, and radio coverage and disseminates information about current health topics via publications such as *HealthLink* and *AIDS-Link* and an annual international conference. Its Web site offers links to relevant information sources.

Illinois Vaccine Awareness Coalition (IVAC)

PO Box 946, Oak Park, IL 60303
(847) 836-0488
e-mail: info@vaccineawareness.org
Web site: www.vaccineawareness.org

IVAC's mission is to educate people on vaccines—their ingredients, contraindications, warnings, adverse reactions, studies, statistics, and legality—for informed vaccine choice. Its goals are to protect children and to prevent vaccine deaths, brain injuries, and physical disabilities. IVAC recommends that people read the vaccine package inserts before they subject themselves or their children to oral, injectable, or nasal-spray vaccines, and the coalition opposes a vaccine registry or any method of surveillance. Its Web site makes a variety of reports and news articles available to its visitors.

Immunization Action Coalition (IAC)

1573 Selby Ave. #234, St. Paul, MN   55104
(651) 647-9009 • fax: (651) 647-9131
e-mail: admin@immunize.org
Web site: www.immunize.org

IAC works to increase immunization rates and prevent disease by creating and distributing educational materials for health professionals and the public that enhance the delivery of safe and effective immunization services. IAC also facilitates communication about the safety, efficacy, and use of vaccines within the broad immunization community of patients, parents, health care organizations, and government health agencies. The organization publishes two semiannual newsletters, *Needle Tips* and *Vaccinate Adults*, and a yearly newsletter, *Vaccinate Women*, for health professionals. Its Web site maintains a large library of technical information and medical opinion resources available to the public.

International Task Force for Disease Eradication (ITFDE)

The Carter Center, One Copenhill, 453 Freedom Pkwy.
Atlanta, GA   30307
(404) 420-5100
e-mail: carterweb@emory.edu
Web site: www.cartercenter.org

ITFDE is one of the health programs of the Carter Center, an organization partnered with Emory University to promote peace, prevent conflict, and improve health across the world. The main goals of the task force are to review progress in the field of disease eradication, review the status of selected diseases for control or eradication, and make recommendations regarding opportunities for eradication or better control of certain diseases. ITFDE is currently making efforts to eradicate Guinea Worm by 2009, a decision sanctioned by the World Health Organization. Health program publications are available on the centers' Web site.

International Union Against Tuberculosis and Lung Disease (The Union)
68 Boulevard Saint Michel, Paris   75006
   France
+33 1 4432 0360 • fax: +33 1 4329 9087
e-mail: union@iuatld.org
Web site: www.iuatld.org

The mission of the Union is to prevent and control tuberculosis and lung disease worldwide, especially in low-income countries. It develops, implements, and assesses antituberculosis and respiratory health programs by gathering and disseminating knowledge of all aspects of tuberculosis and lung disease, including HIV and resulting community health problems; informing doctors, decision makers, opinion leaders, and the general public of the dangers presented by tuberculosis and lung disease and the community health problems associated with them; and coordinating, assisting, and promoting the work of partner projects throughout the world. It publishes the *IJTLD, the International Journal of Tuberculosis and Lung Disease*, which can be accessed via the Union's Web site.

Keep Antibiotics Working
PO Box 14590, Chicago, IL   60614
(773) 525-4952
Web site: www.keepantibioticsworking.com

Keep Antibiotics Working is a coalition of health, consumer, agricultural, environmental, humane, and other advocacy groups dedicated to eliminating a major cause of antibiotic resistance: the inappropriate use of antibiotics in food animals. Its mission is threefold: 1) phasing out use in nonsick animals of antibiotics that are or may become important to human medicine; 2) restricting use in sick animals of antibiotics essential for treating sick humans; and 3) ensuring policy makers and the public will have adequate data at their disposal to track antibiotic use and the development of antibiotic resistance. Available on its Web site is a document library that presents evidence for the misuse of antibiotics.

Malaria Foundation International (MFI)
2120 Spencers Way, Stone Mountain, GA   30087
Web site: www.malaria.org

MFI facilitates the development and implementation of solutions to the health, economic, and social problems caused by malaria. MFI supports partners working to ensure the distribution of long-lasting insecticide-treated bed nets, indoor residual spraying, or effective malaria medications, along with other measures that may be appropriate for specific communities—especially to help children, pregnant women, and people with compromised immune systems. MFI also advocates education and training, with a view toward enhancing economic development and the overall quality of life in malaria-ridden parts of the world. Visitors to its Web site can find educational materials about the disease and relevant news articles.

National Foundation for Infectious Diseases (NFID)
4733 Bethesda Ave. #750, Bethesda, MD   20814
(301) 656-0003 • fax: (301) 907-0878
e-mail: info@nfid.org
Web site: www.nfid.org

NFID is dedicated to educating the public and health care professionals about the causes, treatment, and prevention of infectious diseases. NFID runs a variety of disease prevention and control programs, including STOP Meningitis, Wipe out the Whoop, and the Childhood Influenza Immunization Coalition. Its Web site is a resource of information about infectious diseases, with a library of publications, fact sheets, and links to other organizations.

Project Concern (PCI)
5151 Murphy Canyon Rd. #320, San Diego, CA   92123
(858) 279-9690 • fax: (858) 694-0294
e-mail: postmaster@projectconcern.org
Web site: www.projectconcern.org

PCI's mission is to prevent disease, improve community health, and promote sustainable development. It takes an integrated approach to achieving a lasting impact in the communities it serves. Its programs address factors such as access to nutritious food and clean water, education, gender equity, and economic empowerment. The organization works by providing communities with the tools and resources they need to deliver and sustain effective programs. The scope of its projects reaches more than three million people a year, in eleven different countries. It publishes a newsletter, *Concern News*, three times a year, which is available on the PCI Web site.

Water and Sanitation Program (WSP)
1818 H St. NW, Washington, DC   20433
e-mail: wsp@worldbank.org
Web site: www.wsp.org

WSP is a multidonor partnership of the World Bank. Its goal is to help the poor gain sustained access to improved water supply and sanitation services by working directly with governments at the local and national levels in twenty-seven countries. Its aim is to achieve the Millennium Development Goals of halving the proportion of people without access to safe drinking water and adequate sanitation by 2015. It strives to replicate successful approaches, continue targeted learning efforts, and support reforms that will ensure the adoption of sustainable investments that help people rise from poverty. The program's annual reports and other publications can be accessed on its Web site.

World Health Organization (WHO)
Avenue Appia 20, CH-1211, Geneva 27
  Switzerland
+41 22 791-2111 • fax: +41 22 791-3111
e-mail: info@who.int
Web site: www.who.int

WHO is the directing and coordinating authority for health within the United Nations system. Founded in 1948, it has been responsible for providing leadership on global health matters, shaping the health research agenda, setting norms and standards, articulating evidence-based policy options, providing technical support to countries, and monitoring and assessing health trends. WHO publishes many health reports, assessments, and recommendations, as well as peer-reviewed journals for international and regional audiences on topics ranging from health issues facing developing countries to epidemiological studies and updates on drug research and technology, all available on its Web site.

Bibliography of Books

Thomas Abraham — *Twenty-First-Century Plague: The Story of SARS.* Baltimore: Johns Hopkins University Press, 2005.

Chinua Akukwe — *Don't Let Them Die: HIV/AIDS, TB, Malaria and the Healthcare Crisis in Africa.* London: Adonis & Abbey, 2006.

Arthur Allen — *Vaccine: The Controversial Story of Medicine's Greatest Lifesaver.* New York: Norton, 2007.

Owen Barder et al., eds. — *Making Markets for Vaccines: Ideas to Action.* Washington, DC: Center for Global Development, 2005.

Charles L. Briggs — *Stories in the Time of Cholera: Racial Profiling During a Medical Nightmare.* Berkeley and Los Angeles: University of California Press, 2003.

James Colgrove — *State of Immunity: The Politics of Vaccination in Twentieth-Century America.* Berkeley and Los Angeles: University of California Press, 2006.

Joel Fleishman — *The Foundation: A Great American Secret; How Private Wealth Is Changing the World.* Cambridge, MA: Perseus, 2007.

Robert Fortuine — *Must We All Die? Alaska's Enduring Struggle with Tuberculosis.* Fairbanks: University of Alaska Press, 2005.

Matthew Gandy and Alimuddin Zumla, eds.	*The Return of the White Plague: Global Poverty and the "New" Tuberculosis.* London: Verso, 2003.
Connie Goldsmith	*Invisible Invaders: Dangerous Infectious Diseases.* Minneapolis: Twenty-First-Century Books, 2006.
Denise Grady	*Deadly Invaders: Virus Outbreaks Around the World, from Marburn Fever to Avian Flu.* Boston: Kingfisher, 2006.
Norbert Gualde	*Resistance: The Human Struggle Against Infection.* Trans. Steven Rendall. Washington, DC: Dana Press, 2006.
Mark Harrison	*Disease and the Modern World, 1500 to the Present Day.* Cambridge, UK: Polity Press, 2004.
Thomas Hausler	*Viruses vs. Superbugs: A Solution to the Antibiotics Crisis?* New York: Macmillan, 2008.
Philip Hilts	*Rx for Survival: Why We Must Rise to the Global Health Challenge.* New York: Penguin, 2005.
Mark Honigsbaum	*The Fever Trail: In Search of the Cure for Malaria.* New York: Picador, 2003.
Ichiro Kawachi and Sarah Wamala, eds.	*Globalization and Health.* New York: Oxford University Press, 2007.

Ruth Levine — *Case Studies in Global Health: Millions Saved.* Boston: Jones & Bartlett, 2007.

Elinor Levy and Mark Fischetti — *The New Killer Diseases: How the Alarming Evolution of Mutant Germs Threatens Us All.* New York: Crown, 2003.

Kurt Link — *Understanding New, Resurgent, and Resistant Diseases: How Man and Globalization Create and Spread Illness.* Westport, CT: Praeger, 2007.

Edward Marriott — *Plague: A Story of Science, Rivalry, and the Scourge That Won't Go Away.* New York: Metropolitan, 2002.

Maryn McKenna — *Beating Back the Devil: On the Front Lines with the Disease Detectives of the Epidemic Intelligence Service.* New York: Free Press, 2004.

Cynthia A. Needham and Richard Canning — *Global Disease Eradication: The Race for the Last Child.* Washington, DC: ASM Press, 2003.

Paul A. Offit — *Vaccinated: One Man's Quest to Defeat the World's Deadliest New Diseases.* New York: HarperCollins, 2007.

Richard S. Ostfeld, Felicia Keesing, and Valerie T. Eviner, eds. — *Infectious Disease Ecology: Effects of Ecosystems on Disease and of Disease on Ecosystems.* Princeton: Princeton University Press, 2008.

Charlotte Roberts and Jane Buikstra — *The Bioarchaeology of Tuberculosis: A Global View on a Reemerging Disease.* Gainesville: University Press of Florida, 2008.

Fiammetta Rocco — *Quinine: Malaria and the Quest for a Cure That Changed the World.* New York: HarpersCollins, 2003.

Jessica Snyder Sachs — *Good Germs, Bad Germs: Health and Survival in a Bacterial World.* New York: Hill & Wang, 2007.

Sebastio Salgado — *The End of Polio: A Global Effort to Eradicate Disease.* New York: Bullfinch, 2003.

Abigail A. Salyers and Dixie D. Whitt — *Revenge of the Microbes: How Bacterial Resistance Is Undermining the Antibiotic Miracle.* Washington, DC: ASM Press, 2005.

Irwin W. Sherman — *Twelve Diseases That Changed Our World.* Washington, DC: ASM Press, 2007.

Eileen Stillwaggon — *AIDS and the Ecology of Poverty.* New York: Oxford University Press, 2006.

John W. Ward and Christian Warren, eds. — *Silent Victories: The History and Practice of Public Health in Twentieth-Century America.* New York: Oxford University Press, 2007.

Abigail Woods — *A Manufactured Plague: The History of Foot-and-Mouth Disease in Britain.* Sterling, VA: Earthscan, 2004.

Alan Zelicoff and   *Microbe: Are We Ready for the Next*
Michael Bellomo   *Plague?* New York: AMACOM, 2005.

Index